CASE STUDIES IN
CULTURAL ANTHROPOLOGY

GENERAL EDITORS
George and Louise Spindler
STANFORD UNIVERSITY

DAYTOP VILLAGE
A Therapeutic Community

DAYTOP VILLAGE

A Therapeutic Community

By
BARRY SUGARMAN
Marathon House, Inc.

HOLT, RINEHART AND WINSTON, INC.
NEW YORK CHICAGO SAN FRANCISCO ATLANTA
DALLAS MONTREAL TORONTO LONDON SYDNEY

Library of Congress Cataloging in Publication Data

Sugarman, Barry, 1939–
Daytop Village: a therapeutic community.

(Case studies in cultural anthropology)
Bibliography: p. 133
1. Daytop Village, inc. 2. Narcotic addicts—
Rehabilitation—New York (City) 3. Drug abuse—
Treatment—New York (City) I. Series.
[DNLM: 1. Drug addiction—Rehabilitation.
2. Therapeutic community. WM270 S947d 1974]
HV5833.N45S9 362.2'93'0974726 73–7922
ISBN: 0–03–086291–4

Printed in the United States of America

4 5 6 7 059 9 8 7 6 5 4 3 2 1

Foreword

ABOUT THE SERIES

These case studies in cultural anthropology are designed to bring to students, in beginning and intermediate courses in the social sciences, insights into the richness and complexity of human life as it is lived in different ways and in different places. They are written by men and women who have lived in the societies they write about and who are professionally trained as observers and interpreters of human behavior. The authors are also teachers, and in writing their books they have kept the students who will read them foremost in their minds. It is our belief that when an understanding of ways of life very different from one's own is gained, abstractions and generalizations about social structure, cultural values, subsistence techniques, and the other universal categories of human social behavior become meaningful.

ABOUT THE AUTHOR

Barry Sugarman, Ph.D., Director of Research at Marathon House, Inc., is the author of four books and numerous articles in the fields of sociology, education, and therapeutic communities. He grew up in England, earned a Ph.D. in sociology from Princeton University, and worked for six years at the Farmington Trust Research Unit in Oxford, England, before joining Marathon House. Dr. Sugarman has worked in therapeutic communities in England and the U.S.A. and has taught at Oxford and Princeton Universities, as well as at Southern Illinois, the University of New Hampshire, and the University of Rhode Island. His latest book is *The School and Moral Development*, published by Croom Helm in London and by Barnes & Noble in New York.

ABOUT THE BOOK

Daytop Village is a case study of a therapeutic community consisting of about 100 persons in a large mansion overlooking Prince's Bay on Staten Island. It was established in 1963 and is a part of a movement of broader scope, the purpose of which is to help drug addicts to establish new values and life styles which do not entail drug dependence or the stealing, deceit, and lying which accompany it. Former drug addicts staff the program and continue to help themselves by helping others. The success rate for this therapeutic community is very impressive when results are compared to other drug programs. The therapeutic "method" seems to work. This case study describes how it works and even, to a modest degree, why it works.

The implications of this case study extend far beyond the subject of therapy for drug addicts. Daytop Village is a culture and an institution that exists to change people. It is an educational institution in the broadest sense. Unlike most educational institutions, including schools, prisons, and mental hospitals, it does not, apparently, sabotage its own purposes by a sharp separation of the peer group—those supposedly being taught, and the power group—those supposedly doing the teaching. Daytop culture contains within it certain mechanisms whereby the staff keeps control over informal groups to ensure that they do not function in a negative manner. These mechanisms are described in detail by Dr. Sugarman.

Certain features of the Daytop culture stand out as being particularly important. Confrontation is a pervasive and characteristic feature. A person who is doing wrong by Daytop norms (no matter how insignificant this wrongdoing may appear to an outsider) will be directly confronted by his fellows and told what they disapprove of. These statements imply that Daytop culture is also highly disciplined and conformity-demanding and this is correct.

The important reciprocal feature of Daytop culture—balancing the discipline, conformity, and confrontation—is mutual concern among its members and the warmth of a close fraternal group. Rules are enforced; discipline is maintained. Confrontations occur out of concern. Violations of rules and breaches in discipline are seen as symptoms of the underlying character problems that brought the member to the point of apparently hopeless drug addiction. The concern is to help the person to cope with these problems more effectively so that drugs are no longer necessary.

There are many other specific features of Daytop culture and cultural transmission processes that are described by Dr. Sugarman in this case study. One other deserves mention here, and that is the Puritan Ethic. Within the framework of the Daytop Concept one learns to be responsible. One learns to face up to the consequences of one's behavior. One learns that it is necessary to work for what one receives. There is no "free lunch."

Thre is much in the culture of Daytop Village that is reminiscent of an earlier American culture. The emphasis upon work, upon concern for others, and upon egalitarianism all seem familiar to Americans imbued with the old traditions and values. It is interesting in this context that Daytop Village at one recent point in its evolution started to become a form of radical social movement. Life within the therapeutic community became not merely a preparation for life outside, but an answer to it. The self-seeking materialism and social isolation of the society outside came to be seen as inferior to the values of concern and honesty operating within Daytop. In this respect Daytop Village and other therapeutic communities referred to by Dr. Sugarman are similar to intentional societies or communitarian movements.

GEORGE AND LOUISE SPINDLER
General Editors

San Diego, Spain

Preface

One of the most fascinating social developments in the U.S.A. today is the growth and proliferation of therapeutic communities, where former drug addicts are living and struggling together to gain a new, drug-free outlook on life. These communities are tightly regulated and run, not by university-trained or board-certified professionals but mainly by former addicts who have come up through the same kind of program and have shown an aptitude for this kind of work.

Daytop Village, the subject of this study, was established in 1963 and is one of the earlier and more influential of these communities; not, we note, the earliest. That honor belongs to the California-based organization known as Synanon, which truly "invented" this novel form of social organization with no assistance from professionals or governmental agencies and in the face of a good deal of opposition or indifference. Although Synanon has been the subject of at least three books (Casriel, 1963; Endore, 1968; Yablonsky, 1965) it has not yet been analyzed in the way this study attempts to analyze Daytop—examining systematically how it operates as a social organization and how the processes of individual change on the part of members are fostered by the social structure and group process. In this important sense then this study is unique.

The significance of the Synanon–Daytop type of social organization for modern society is profound and it is manifold. It is the most successful approach to the problem of rehabilitating drug addicts so far available, and it can also be applied to the resocialization of people who practice other forms of delinquent or self-destructive behavior. As such it could revitalize the whole field of the helping professions, given the right conditions.

This wider effect on the helping services is not going to come overnight, of course, but already the influence of Daytop in the field of treatment and rehabilitation of addicts has been profound. Even in 1968–1969 a survey sponsored by the National Institute of Mental Health found forty treatment programs for addicts that described themselves as "therapeutic communities," sixty-two employing ex-addicts, and ten headed by an ex-addict. The one program which had the greatest direct influence on these newer programs is Daytop, being located in the New York area at the center of the greatest concentration of drug addicts in the nation and having some official sponsorship and acceptance from the start.

Thus we may say that this study of Daytop not only has intrinsic interest as a case study of the culture and the sociological and psychological processes which operate in this type of therapeutic community; it is further a key to understanding a movement which has already become important in the fields of treatment and rehabilitation, because Daytop played a major historical role in the genesis of that movement.

On one level, these tightly structured communal groups represent a serious challenge to the values of modern western civilization. They are at odds with the secular values on one point, emphasizing group solidarity over individual freedom, but Daytop, Synanon, and similar communities display a more marked devotion than does the rest of society as a whole to three other supposed values of our Judaeo-Christian heritage. We refer to the values of honesty in personal relationships, altruistic concern for each other, and the Puritan ethic that a person should enjoy only that for which he has striven.

Visitors to Daytop and to the other communities which truly embody the great "Concept" developed at Synanon, seldom fail to remark upon these features of the group. Many have felt attracted by this way of life with its apparent honesty, mutual concern, and responsibility and they have sought to associate themselves with the group—by donating supplies or cash, by becoming regular visitors to the house, or, in the case of those employed in the helping professions, by trying to apply the "Concept" approach in their own work, and in a few instances by finding jobs within these groups as they started to broaden the base of their staff recruitment. The author of this study is one such professional who has made that shift of career by joining Marathon House, Inc., an organization operating similar kinds of therapeutic communities in the New England region. Marathon House grew directly from Daytop in the sense that its founder, Jim Germano, was an early Daytop graduate and a senior member before moving to Rhode Island in 1967 to establish Marathon House.

My first contact with Daytop was in 1967. I had been doing research on the sociology of schools and other socializing agencies when some friends took me to visit Daytop Village. We visited the Staten Island house where a resident sat down with me for an hour or so and explained some of the basic facts about Daytop. My first response to this visit was one of great intellectual fascination and excitement, though quite different feelings were to develop on further acquaintance. I went away and wrote a short article that focused on the mechanics and formal structure of Daytop, for that was what most impressed me at that stage (Sugarman, 1967).

Soon I returned to spend five days as a resident, though a privileged one. This time it was the friendliness and warmth and the feeling of emotional security in the group that made the greatest impression on me—the feeling that this collection of one-hundred people was in some true sense a "family."

The other outstanding impression for me this time was how hard it was to live up to the standards of this group. A year later (1968) I returned to spend two months as a resident. This time I was able to make a contribution to the educational program in Daytop by running discussion groups on current affairs and other subjects of general interest, but for most of my time I was living as a resident, subject to the same rules and controls. The impressions of the previous year were reinforced, and in addition I began to see some of the very subtle mechanisms operating below the surface on which the social integration of this remarkable community depends.

The following account is based mainly on observational data collected as a participant in the two months of summer 1968. Further visits in 1969 and 1970 enabled me to deepen the analysis in certain areas of the investigation, including a follow-up on the progress and aftermath of a serious crisis which will be discussed in the last chapter of this book. Apart from the participant-observer data, certain other sources are also used: official records kept for Daytop's own purposes (mainly daily logs); statistics compiled in the research department of Daytop at the time of fieldwork and later (1972); some tape-recordings of speeches made under Daytop auspices; the final project report to N.I.M.H. by Joseph Shelly, kindly made available to me by Walter V. Collier, Director of Research, Daytop Village, Inc.; and retrospective interviews with several Daytop graduates now associated with Marathon House. These interviews gave me some new and significant insights, for which I am grateful to Felix Donowa, Richie Rode, and Jim Germano.

Thanks are also owed to O. Hobart Mowrer, Sherwin Feinhandler, and Sharon Sugarman for reading earlier drafts of this book and helping to improve it with some valuable criticisms. Lastly I want to express my gratitude to the members of Daytop who accepted me and taught me so much. My involvement with Daytop Village was a sorely needed turning point in my own life. Writing now, two years later, I think it is possible to present a balanced account of this community—not a totally dispassionate one, but one which oscillates between the perspective of the participants (biased admittedly towards the official definitions of situations) and the perspective of the social scientist. To repeat a point made earlier, this is not an exotic culture having a purely academic interest; nor is it merely a rehabilitation agency with relevance to the human service professions; rather it has important implications for all of us who live in western society and who are at all aware of the value crisis in which we live.

The present tense, as used in this book, refers to the years 1967 and 1968 when most of the fieldwork was done. Most of the writing was done after I came to work at Marathon House. Here I have had the opportunity to develop my ideas in the environment of a therapeutic community that combines the best of the Daytop model with some new and evolving ideas. For this congenial setting I am grateful to my colleagues and especially to our executive director Jim Germano.

BARRY SUGARMAN

Providence, Rhode Island
October, 1973

Contents

1 / Introduction

WELCOME TO DAYTOP

Overlooking Prince's Bay on Staten Island stands a large, white mansion, built around the turn of the century. It was originally the home of a wealthy family, then it passed into the ownership of a religious order. Today (1967–1968) its ownership is indicated by a signboard, standing at the foot of the drive which curves gracefully uphill to the front entrance. The black letters on the white board read: "Daytop Village: A New Direction in Helping Man To Help Himself." In Daytop Village former drug addicts are being helped and are helping each other to establish new values and life styles that do not entail drug dependence or the stealing, deceit, and lying that accompany it. This is a drug-free community.

Entering the house, one finds a large hall dominated by a large, curving, wooden staircase. Seated at a desk in the center of this hall is a young person who greets the visitor and asks to know his business. Other young men and women, who evidently live here, pass to and fro through this area. Some come from down a passageway that leads straight back, carrying cups of coffee. They may be headed toward the large living room or lounge which lies directly off the front hall to the left. There, depending on the time of day, others can be seen playing cards, talking, and listening to music. At other times of the day a work crew can be seen cleaning the room. Occasionally the living room will be packed with eighty to ninety people while some kind of meeting is in progress. At all times, though, someone is watching the front door for visitors.

Located beneath the large stairwell is an office, separated from the busy front hall by only a half-door, rising to chest height. Over the top of this door can be seen a telephone switchboard and its operator. In addition, there is at most times at least one other person in this office, looking out to see what is happening in the front area, making and receiving calls on the intercom, and—as one listens it becomes apparent—giving orders. If the visitor is new or not known to the person sitting at the front desk, the latter will turn to this office for help in checking the visitor's credentials.

The visitor will be asked to sign the visitor's log book at the front desk. While he is waiting there for his clearance or for the person he is to see to appear, he will probably notice that residents who enter or leave through the front door check in and out at the front desk. Upon request, the person manning the desk places or removes a small, colored tag on a board bearing a long list of names. What is the reason for this careful scrutiny of visitors and for the checking in and out of residents? There are several: the staff administering the house often need to know where someone is, ex–drug addicts need to be kept under careful surveillance lest they seek and find ways to evade the strict no-drug rules of the house, and visitors must be screened for the protection of residents. Drug pushers, former cronies of residents, and even their family members who are not drug users are all unwelcome as they are likely to undermine the progress that residents are making. Relatives are likely to upset a resident's progress more from misguided good intentions, but nonetheless, they are not free to visit except by special permission.

If the visitor is likely to have to wait more than a couple of minutes for the person he wants to see, another resident who happens to pass through the hall or someone who is sitting in the adjacent living room will be detailed by the person in charge of the front desk to entertain him (the visitor) in the meantime. He will be offered the ritual cup of coffee and will be taken somewhere to sit down, usually into the dining room.

There, as they talk, the visitor will probably notice signs of busy activity in the kitchen, which adjoins the dining room, as the kitchen crew prepares the next meal or cleans up from the last one, or both at the same time.

The visitor will probably be asked what brings him to Daytop and encouraged to ask any questions that he may have about it. The resident will, given half a chance, talk expansively about the routines and philosophy of Daytop, explaining that it is a self-help community of former drug addicts; that they do all their own work themselves, their own cooking, cleaning, maintenance, and so forth; that their staff are themselves former drug addicts who have come up through the program themselves and proved their ability to help themselves and others; that Daytop should not be regarded as a "program" but more as a family of people helping each other to overcome their problems; that drugs themselves were not their real problem but only the symptom of underlying problems of personality, and especially the problem of not feeling good about oneself.

The resident will also talk about himself with the kind of simple directness and openness that is uncommon in most segments of modern western societies. He may talk about how he came to be in Daytop; about being in trouble with the law, frankly naming his crimes—typically larceny, robbery, drug offenses, forgery, prostitution; about abusing and preying upon his family until (often) they threw him out; about how close he has been to dying from O.D.'s (overdoses); about how he thought Daytop would be easier than jail, the typical motivation for a new resident. He will not talk about his drug habit in any detail, as this is not allowed. But, time permitting, he will probably talk about what he has learned about himself since coming into Daytop and how his picture of himself has started to change; about the gratifications which he is finding in this group and in the feeling of closeness and mutual concern which is generated. If he is being really open, the resident will admit that he still yearns for his old life at times and sometimes feels like "splitting." Partly this is a reaction to the heavy and seemingly endless demands that are made on one in Daytop; partly too, though, it is because a person still retains a large amount of "negative" desires in him even after (say) a year of the

Daytop Village on Staten Island, approaching the house from driveway.

"positive" influence of Daytop and after his most conscientious efforts to do what is expected.

As they sit talking, the visitor and the Daytop resident, the visitor will probably notice that the resident is very careful not to drop cigarette ash on the floor or table and carefully picks it up if any should drop. He also painstakingly wipes up any drops of coffee. When they leave the table, he removes his cup, asks the guest to do likewise, empties the ash tray, and leaves the chairs straight. All visible parts of the house are cleaned, dusted, painted, and polished immaculately. Two things that are not seen are full ashtrays or brimming garbage cans.

In the course of my introduction to Daytop and to some of its residents, it was made clear to me in no uncertain terms that my initial practice of writing notes in a small notebook while I talked with residents and staff was severely frowned upon. I did not dare to broach the possibility of tape-recording these conversations. The notes that I do have were written from memory anywhere between half an hour and several hours later. Even at the time they were written I was painfully aware that I had forgotten parts of what was said. In the following quotation, therefore, I have combined parts of my notes of several different conversations in order to illustrate the very moving frankness and openness one hears from Daytop residents, even as a stranger to their house.

> I've been shooting dope for five years. Dope was my whole life—getting high and stealing enough so I'd have money to buy dope. I never cared about nothing or nobody—not even myself. Certainly not myself. I lived in filthy basements and hallways. No one cared about me. Maybe my family did once but I just kept on stealing from them until they threw me out because they couldn't take it no more. I had no friends—just some other dope-fiends I would shoot up with. I had been in jail a few times. I've been in the Rockefeller program but that is just like jail. It didn't do me no good. Then I met this guy I used to cop with in my old neighborhood. He looked different. He looked straight. He was in Daytop and working at the SPAN storefront. [SPAN is the Daytop induction center.] So he talked to me about Daytop and got me to come along here. Man, I was real tired of that whole scene out there and I didn't know what to do. Like, this place is really something else. I really care about the people here—a lot of them, the ones I've got to know. And they really care about me. That was even harder to accept—that people really could care about me. I feel bad when I mess up—do something wrong and hurt someone else because I never stopped to think. I never used to be like that. I never cared. Now I've got a real family—somewhere I feel like I belong. I'm responsible for the newer brothers and sisters in the house and I have to act like a role model for them—the same as others did for me when I was new here. We have a saying, "You can only keep it if you give it away." That means your new values, your self-respect, your good feelings. You have to give them away to other people all the time, or else you lose what you already got for yourself.

IMPRESSIONS AND STATISTICS

Soon after entering Daytop, the visitor starts to form some definite impressions as to what kind of place this is. One impression that may be formed in only half an hour is of a well-ordered community where rules are generally respected and enforced when necessary, where people jump to carry out orders and do so quite cheerfully, and where people work hard. Considering the kind of people who live here and what they were like before, things seem to run with amazing smoothness. As one sees more, one discovers that this orderliness is only achieved at the price of constant pressure and surveillance, tough sanctions for deviance, and a high dropout rate.

A second impression develops more slowly and only as one gets a more intimate look at life in Daytop. On a superficial level this impression is one of group solidarity. It is also one of openness and readiness to welcome the new member or even the visitor and to extend oneself to make him feel part of the group. On further acquaintance one discovers the great amount of warmth, concern, and love that flows between many of those who live here.

One sees this side of Daytop especially after work is over, when residents sit talking informally. Anyone who is upset over something will be encouraged to talk about it; he will be given advice usually based on similar experiences and moral support in the reassurance that he is capable of coping with the problem himself with the help of his fellow residents. The person giving out the advice can usually say, "I know how you are feeling. I used to feel like that all the time. I still do a lot. But I learned that I have to handle it a different way. It's no good taking it the way you are and the way I used to. You have to . . . Then you can live with yourself a whole lot easier. I did it though it's still hard for me, and you can too." The new resident will also get reassurance that he can count on the help of his peers here in Daytop. These talks may go on late into the night—especially on the three nights each week when encounter groups are held for residents to pour out their grievances against each other (as noisily and abusively as they please) and to hear their peers point out to them with great forcefulness the behavior they must change. After these sessions a special closeness is usually evident: bad feelings between residents have been aired and they come to realize that they want very much to get along better; all who have been talked to in the encounter have experienced the concern of the others to help them and those who have really been open have, by their openness, expressed trust in the others; even those who received only unwelcome criticism and got "hit over the head with a load of reality" are "patched up," both in the session and afterwards, so they will not feel rejected by their peers.

These impressions of Daytop are not peculiar to this observer but evidently are shared by other visitors with whom I have talked. They should be taken seriously since they do hold up and tend to be validated by further observation. Daytop staff, and therefore other residents too, feel strongly that anyone who is interested in knowing what Daytop is all about should find out by "getting involved" on a personal level; by talking with residents, by living in the house—in short, by collecting impressions, not by collecting statistics.

From the social scientist's viewpoint, though, there are certain aspects of the functioning of a group such as this which can only be assessed through the use of statistics. Such aspects would include: size of membership, rate of admission of new members, and numbers of members lost at different time periods. It is pointless to argue whether data of this kind are more important than data of the impressionistic kind, or vice-versa. The point is that each serves a different function and that together they may complement each other. Daytop staff are taking a position against the kind of investigator who wants to know only the statistical data without bothering to find out anything about the subjective aspects of the group to which it applies. When I had demonstrated my good faith by spending five days living in Daytop and being involved on what was evidently considered a personal level in the group's activities, then they were willing to let me have access to statistical data, too.

These data are important for this study in two ways. First, they allow us to establish the fact that a certain proportion of those who enter Daytop do complete the program and live drug-free lives for a certain time thereafter. In other words, what is at issue here is whether Daytop is actually bringing about change in the individuals who pass through it; whether we are looking at a group with a remarkable communal way of life which has no lasting effect on its individual members when they leave or whether we are looking at a group with a remarkable, communal way of life which also has a lasting socializing effect on its members—not just a community but a specifically "therapeutic" community.

On this point Daytop statistics show that up to July 1968, forty-five persons had been "confirmed" as having honorably completed the treatment program and being considered fit to make all their own personal decisions from now on. A further thirty who left prematurely (in the view of Daytop staff) were nonetheless known to be drug-free. Two of the forty-five confirmees were known to have failed by relapsing to drug use—at least temporarily. Unfortunately these statistics which were made available to me in 1968 do not specify a definite time period after confirmation over which the relapse or nonrelapse of Daytop "graduates" was observed. They should suffice, however, to establish the fact that Daytop is a *therapeutic* or *rehabilitative* community which brings about certain changes in its members—not *all* of them, but a significant number. What number? Or rather, we may ask, what proportion? This is another question requiring an answer in statistical form.

We can try to answer this question about "success rate" by using some data presented in 1969 on a group of ninety-six of the earliest Daytop residents and a control group of fifty-eight drug offenders on probation. Seven of the Daytop subjects have to be excluded because five of them were still in treatment, one died in Daytop, and one vanished without trace. Out of the remaining eighty-nine, thirty-one (or 35 percent) were deemed successful, in terms of no further illegal drug use, gainful employment, and staying out of jail. Among the control group only 4 percent were deemed successful—and even those with some reservations. Clearly, everyone who enters Daytop is not guaranteed to leave as a success. But

The Daytop "Phoenix," sculpted by an earlier resident, stands in front of the house.

even a success rate of 35 percent (with a failure rate of 65 percent) has to be considered impressive when dealing with drug addicts. Among the ninety-six who entered Daytop, the average length of addiction was five years (Shelly, 1969).

Statistics are also important to this study in order to establish some of the basic parameters of group structure and process. First, we can determine the size of the population at Daytop Village (Staten Island). On July 24, 1968, it numbered 100 persons, including paid staff and residents at all stages of treatment. This method of enumerating the house population is, in itself, an interesting datum. It is found in the so-called "population sheet" issued weekly from the business office of the house, which lists the names of all residents and staff in order of date of entry, with date noted along side the name. The only other datum to appear here is the New York City borough from which the Daytop resident hails.

Second, we can determine the number of residents who have been in the house for different lengths of time at any given point in time. Again, on July 24, 1968 this was as follows:

Over 24 months	11
Over 18 months, up to 24	18
Over 12 months, up to 18	13
Over 6 months, up to 12	18
Over 3 months, up to 6	26
Up to 3 months	14

The fact that this age structure deviates from the classical pyramid structure, so commonly found, calls attention to the fact that the Staten Island house is the residence for reentry of persons from *both* of the Daytop houses (Swan Lake and Staten Island) who are working in the SPAN storefront centers in Manhattan. They are, of course, entirely from the top two or three age categories as they begin their "reentry" into outside society.

Third, certain process parameters of this organization may be statistically defined. Over the two-year period from January 1, 1965, to December 31, 1966, there were 303 admissions, averaging twelve or thirteen per month. "Splits" or unauthorized departures were tallied for a seven-month period (January to July 1968). Ranging between three and twenty-five per month, the average was just about twelve splits per month. Unless either the split rate was lower in the latter half of the year, or the admission rate was higher, therefore, the net growth rate of this house in terms of population must have been not more than one person per month. Actual month by month population figures were not obtained.

Again, we may express statistically the drop-out process in terms of the proportion of residents who drop out ("split") at given intervals. In the first thirty days after admission, 25 percent of new residents split; a further 16 percent leave between the second and sixth month inclusive, and a further 5 percent in the second half of the year.

HOW IT STARTED

At the time of this study Daytop Village was a thriving therapeutic community of some one hundred souls in Staten Island plus another one hundred forty in the sister house in Swan Lake (upstate New York). It all began, though, as a shaky experiment of the Probation Department of the Kings County Supreme Court of New York State. In 1963, the first year of operation, the project could not even begin to meet the quota of twenty-five residents in treatment. The split rate was too high, discipline was too loose, and the feeling of purposefulness that was so evident in 1967–1968 was not yet established.

The original experimental project, funded for five years initially by the National Institute of Mental Health, began with high hopes. Its sponsors had recently "discovered" Synanon, the pioneer of this kind of therapeutic community, located in California, and decided that here was the answer for which they had been searching. Drug addicts could at last be helped to stay off drugs through the self-help principle embodied in the community of former addicts living together as a group dedicated to changing not only drug-use behavior but the whole complex of related attitudes that supported it. Synanon was the first group to utilize successfully the social pressures of a closed group or "total institution," not only to modify the behavior of addicts temporarily (while in the group), but also to change their underlying attitudes and hence to modify their behavior on a more enduring basis.

Synanon was a truly innovating organization, created by Charles E. Dederich, a former alcoholic. He was not only familiar with the group dynamics of Alcoholics Anonymous but was an active campaigner for that organization. More or less by chance he found himself leading a group of alcoholics and drug addicts who were squatting in his bachelor apartment. He evolved the noisy form of confrontation group where participants shout and curse their grievances and resentments before settling down to analyze their problems as manifested in *the present*; he developed the harsh verbal reprimand or "haircut" because it suited his personality and he observed that it was effective; members of the group lived together at first because they were homeless but this principle of joint residence became a fundamental rule. Dederich also broke radically with all previous social work traditions by saying (sometimes explicitly, sometimes by implication), "Junkies need Synanon, we don't need them." In line with this, he established the policy of demanding, before accepting them into the house, that they agree to conform to all rules and make some "investment" as a token of sincerity, for example by telephoning at designated times, giving up prized personal possessions, or by doing something difficult but meaningful, such as yelling for help before a group of residents. All of these features of Synanon are reproduced in Daytop and, by now, in many other organizations which model themselves on Synanon, Daytop, or their successors.

Synanon began in 1958. The Daytop Lodge experiment, as it was first known, began in the fall of 1963. It started as a branch of the Probation Department of New York Supreme Court, Second Judicial District (Brooklyn and Staten Island). Chief Probation Officer Joseph A. Shelly was one of the prime movers to establish an innovative program for male drug offenders with felony convictions on probation to his department. Also associated with him were Dr. Alexander Bassin, director of group therapy at the Brooklyn Civic Center Clinic, and Dr. Daniel Casriel, a psychiatrist. These three, accompanied by Professor Herbert A. Bloch, a noted criminologist, toured the country visiting centers of supposed expertise in the handling of drug addicts. Initially their goal was both broad and vague: to initiate some new method of helping drug offenders that would be more effective than the then prevailing routines of incarceration, detoxification, and probation or parole "supervision." Only when they visited Synanon did they decide, with the sudden shock of recognition, that here was the new approach for which they were searching. Casriel returned to spend several weeks in residence at Synanon studying their methods. At the end of his stay he was more than ever convinced that Synanon had found the answer to the problem of treating addicts. Soon afterwards he published a book on Synanon (Casriel, 1963).

Whereas Synanon was then and still is a totally independent organization, receiving no government funds, Daytop was planned to operate in partnership with the state bureaucracy, fully funded. There is great irony in the fact that Synanon, the experts, was not supported by government funds, while organizations with far less experience or proven competence got funded. Later we shall consider some of the reasons for this peculiar situation. For now we merely note it as a fact and note that it has contributed to the considerable bitterness felt by Synanon leaders towards the government agencies in question and towards their imitators who have fared better than they with funding.

Daytop Lodge opened in 1963, not where we found the Village in 1967–1968 but in a smaller building known as "Butler Manor." When the property overlooking Prince's Bay was acquired in 1965, the name of the project was changed from Daytop Lodge to Daytop Village, and it was incorporated as a private, nonprofit corporation. Control was now vested in a board of directors instead of the Probation Department. Whereas this project had initially restricted admission to males and to convicted felons in the care of the Probation Department, admission was now unrestricted by any conditions, save that of the person's need and desire to enter the program and willingness to conform to its demands.

The move to the new premises was strongly opposed by local residents in the vicinity of the new house, as the initial establishment of the house at Butler Manor had also been. There were hostile letters to the local newspaper and pickets at the house. The effects of these demonstrations were for a time to frighten Daytop residents at least as much as their presence in the neighborhood frightened the more fearful neighbors. In the course of time the local opposition faded, and there were no attempts at harassment. Some neighbors eventually visited the house and changed their attitude to having Daytop in their neighborhood.

Daytop came to play an important part in bringing the Synanon approach to the East Coast and in particular to New York City. In the early planning stages of what became the vast Phoenix House program of New York City, Daytop staff played an important role in advising city officials and visits to Daytop were important in convincing them to support a therapeutic community type of program. As plans for the Phoenix program developed, former Synanon personnel were hired, and today comprise the greater part of senior Phoenix House staff.

In its first year Daytop nearly failed due to the difficulties experienced in finding a suitable director and staff. Originally a particular Synanon graduate had agreed to take the job, but due to repeated bureaucratic delays he took a job elsewhere. For a year no one who was at all suitable could be found. Four different directors held the position but not for long. None of them could impose any discipline or keep out contraband: wine, marijuana, etc. At this time many residents were working outside and had plenty of opportunities to acquire contraband.

In October 1964 Daytop changed abruptly from a loosely regulated "half-way house" to a tightly run therapeutic community in which rules were consistently enforced and in which residents were sufficiently identified with the rules and values of the group that they would report each other for nonconforming behavior. It became the kind of community which we found in 1967 and 1968. The new director who made that swift and decisive change was David Deitch, formerly director of the Synanon house in Westport, Connecticut. With him as assistants came two former Synanon colleagues and his wife, not an ex-addict but well-versed in the ways of Synanon. How they went about achieving that decisive change we shall consider in a later chapter.

This phase of Daytop's early life, as a relatively small group under the direct, personal leadership of the intense, eloquent, idealistic Deitch, was already a thing of the past in 1967 and 1968. Then the resident population was already around 250 in two houses; preparations were being made to open a third house; house directorships were in the hands of the first cohort of Daytop graduates—men who had come through those early days with David Deitch as their immediate taskmaster, counselor, friend, and model. The culture of this group as I found it was based as a matter of policy on that of Synanon. But this policy was only realized through the day-by-day management and ministrations of these few key people, Deitch and his "core group" as they came to be known. In our next chapter, "The Daytop Concept," we begin our analysis of the culture of this remarkable community.

2/The Daytop Concept

The "Concept" is the term most often used by Daytop residents and staff to refer to the Daytop community, the Daytop philosophy and ideals, and the Daytop methods of doing things. The "Concept" encompasses all of these aspects at once. They might say, for example, "before I came into the Concept . . ." or "even if I don't work for Daytop eventually I still intend to live the Concept wherever I am" or "John has learned to talk well and give a good impression but Concept-wise he's still got a long way to go."

Let us first examine the procedures a person must go through in order to become a Daytop resident. This will reveal some of the more salient features of the Concept. Then we shall attempt to define more explicitly some of the basic norms and rules that are operative in Daytop.

A "PROSPECT" SEEKS ADMISSION

It is not made easy to become a Daytop resident. In fact, there is a deliberate effort to make it harder than it could be, as a preliminary screening device to eliminate those applicants whose motivation is the weakest. "You need us, we don't need you" is the attitude taken by Daytop leaders towards the applicant (or "prospect"). When a prospect phones, he is usually told to phone again at a specified time, then again. He will have to make a series of such phone calls punctually at the set time before being allowed to come to the house for his interview. Prospects who initially contacted SPAN, the Daytop storefront induction center, have already had their motivation tests. They are given a series of times to call the induction center, then they are interviewed at the center and are expected to attend on a daily basis and participate in the activities of the center. The program of activities there is a light-weight version of the residential Daytop program.

The SPAN office, which is staffed by senior Daytop residents and which runs the induction program as well as certain community action activities in Manhattan's Lower East Side, sends prospects for their interview at the Staten Island house when they have satisfied the requirements of the induction center. In either case, whether the prospect comes through SPAN or directly "from the streets," he is subjected to some initial motivation testing before he even arrives at the Daytop House.

On arrival the testing continues. He is seated on the "prospect chair," which is placed in the front area or lobby of the house, and told that he may not speak to anyone except the residents designated to watch him and must not move from the chair without permission. The prospect will usually sit on the chair for several hours, in full view of all residents as they come and go through this busy front area, seen but not spoken to. He has to ask for cigarettes, to go to the toilet, or anything else he wants. When mealtime comes he is brought a sandwich to eat on "the chair."

It is truly a testing experience. The prospect sees people moving around purposefully, giving and accepting orders, working, socializing, looking clean and tidy. Whatever this group may be—and the prospect is frequently very confused and unclear about this—it is very different from any other "program," hospital, or jail which he may have been in. As he (or she) sits in isolation on the prospect chair, he is decidedly not a part of this group—at this time.

Some prospects lose their nerve and "split," that is they ask for their possessions back and they leave, as they are free to do. Many prospects come to Daytop with an "either-or" proposition from court, which stipulates that either they get accepted into Daytop and stay there or else go to jail. If a person with this kind of stipulation splits, that is *his* problem. Daytop is not a custodial institution with obligations to force people to stay.

The prospect sitting on the chair may see a resident whom he once knew on the street as a fellow addict—perhaps someone he used to get "high" with. The prospect may try to catch the eye of his former buddy and get a nod from him or a wink that says "don't worry, we can make out in this place just like we did on the streets." Instead his former buddy ignores him or stares coldly through him. Daytop residents know they are expected to do this; they know that there are serious consequences if they do not play their role in the expected way in this situation; they know that sharp-eyed staff and fellow residents are watching to see that they behave as expected; and they may know the reason for this rule. The reason is that when a person enters Daytop his loyalty is expected to be transferred from "the streets" and his "junkie" values to the Daytop community and its values of honesty, concern, and responsibility. The former junkie who has entered Daytop and "taken his vows" is supposed to have set his sights in a totally different direction from those of the antisocial, irresponsible, dishonest street junkie that he once was. Each and every Daytop resident is supposed to have crossed a moral divide which separates him from his former way of life and those who are still identified with it. The Daytop resident can be proud of his new identity, which is emphasized by this isolation of the prospect—though it is presumably distasteful to the latter.

Eventually the prospect is brought in for his interview. He enters a room dominated by a large, round coffee table, around which six or eight young adults are seated. They are all dressed very casually; no one wears a tie or jacket. The prospect is told to sit in the one remaining chair around the table. He is treated courteously, thought not very cordially. He is addressed by his first name and may be introduced to the other people present by their first names. There are no files, questionnaires, or notebooks to be seen. This is very different from the usual interview an applicant gets at most social agencies, as the prospect may be thinking to himself.

"What can we do for you?" One of the interviewers asks.

"Why are you here?" asks another.

"What is the matter with you that you have to shoot dope?"

These are some of the questions that are fired at the prospect. If he is the highly verbal, con-man type of junkie who has manipulated social workers quite easily in the past, he may start to spin a web of fabrications along the general line of "I've come to the end of the road . . . I can't stand myself anymore—the way I've been living . . . I'm determined to kick the filthy habit. . . ." The Daytoppers let him go on for a short while, then one of them will stop him short, shouting loudly and angrily,

> Knock off that shit, will you? Who do you think you are talking to? We ain't no bunch of bleeding heart social workers. The people you see here were dope fiends themselves, see? And at one time we all came in here sniveling just like you are doing now—"I want to rid myself of the horrors of drug addiction."

All of the interviewers laugh. This transparent attempt at deception is a standing joke in Daytop.

In this sort of way the Daytop interviewers establish their claim to authority and credibility in the mind of the prospect. They commonly ask him about the nature and extent of his drug habit. This is generally ridiculed—especially if there is any hint of boasting or pride in the amount of drugs he claims to have used, which is quite common. "You seem to think you're some kind of big-time junkie, man. Why the people in here, we *spilled* more dope than you ever shot in your whole life."

Whatever role the prospect starts out trying to play in his interview, he is soon faced with questions which cannot be answered honestly without making himself look bad. Inexorably the interviewers follow a basic strategy which leads eventually to admissions highly damaging to the prospect's former pride. Before he comes into the interview his interrogators know his background and know what facts to focus on in order to cut him down to size. If he has lived with his parents, sponging off them financially and letting his mother cook and clean for him, this will be presented as the situation of a dependent "baby." If he has been to jail for drug offenses and continued "sticking dirty needles in his arm," this is presented as the behavior of a "lunatic" who cannot learn from experience. Similarly if he acknowledges that friends or acquaintances of his have died from overdoses; this is the behavior of a *stupid* person; this is the behavior of a *baby*. These words hit him in the gut. They stick in his throat as he is made to say them in response to the leading questions of his interrogators. Until he does this he cannot be accepted.

> "Why are you here?"
> "Because I'm all fucked up. Because my whole life is a mess."
> "What would you call the kind of person who acts the way you do and does the things you have just told us about?"
> "A stupid person . . . a baby."

When the prospect interview has progressed to this point and some close variation on the above litany has been uttered, the first and major objective is to get the prospect to make an "investment." This is supposed to be a token of the strength of his sincerity in wanting to enter Daytop. If he has long hair, he may be asked to agree to having it closely cropped. He may be asked to scream at the top of his lungs, "Help me" or "I need help."

The function of this mortifying experience is not only to test further the motivation of the prospect, but more importantly to prepare him psychologically for the step he is about to take of entering into a group of people with a culture almost totally oriented to changing his values, attitudes, behavior patterns, and his very self-identity. The interview is an attack on his old self-image as an adult with some serious problems, a victim of misfortune, to a new self-image as an overgrown infant who has never grown up in terms of character development and moral values, as someone *responsible* for what he has done. Whatever misfortunes he may have had in life—such as being born in a slum, having parents who failed to bring him up properly, teachers who mistreated him and so forth—nevertheless *he* is the one who took a needle in his hand and stuck it into his veins; *he* is the one who lied and stole to get money for his habit.

Accepting responsibility for his own behavior, the newcomer to Daytop can set about learning to change it. Accepting his immaturity and the fact that others who were once like him have learned to grow up and live free from drugs through Daytop, he has a reason for accepting the authority of the Daytop rules and its leaders. This authority, as we already have seen, is extensive—it is, in the literal sense of the word, "totalitarian."

When the prospect has satisfied his interviewers the atmosphere in the room changes suddenly. The leader of the interview says "Welcome to Daytop, brother." He gets up from his seat, smiling, and shakes the new resident by the hand. Everyone else does likewise. The sternness of Daytop gives way to let the warmth and comradeship break through. The new resident has to give up all his personal possessions into the custody of "the house" until he earns the "privilege" of having them back one by one. He is told that he may not leave the premises, make or receive phone calls, write or receive letters, again until he has earned these "privileges" by his efforts to comply with the Daytop norms and change himself. After the rigors of the intake interview, these restrictions do not seem so very hard.

One of the interviewers takes charge of the new resident and takes him around to meet his new "family." He is shown around the building and introduced to individual residents. If a large number are present together (for instance, for a meal) the sponsor will call for quiet and say, "I want everyone to meet our new brother, Joe. Let's give him a nice welcome to Daytop." This will lead to loud clapping and cheering of a very friendly kind, after which individuals will come forward and introduce themselves, shaking the new member's hand and practically mobbing him with their welcome.

Some prospects coming to Daytop have already kicked their habit physically whether in hospital, jail, or otherwise, but others still have a habit when they apply for admission. They are warned not to come to the house "high." Upon arrival at the house, the "expediters" who process them will ask if they are carrying any drugs or addicts' paraphernalia with them. They will also ask if they are "high." They will not search them for contraband until after they have passed their interview, but while they wait for it on the prospect chair they will be watched every moment and even escorted to the toilet. The experienced eyes of the expediters will also appraise whether the prospect seems to be high, despite his protestations to the contrary. If he is thought to be high, he may be sent away and told to call again or he may be told to sit on the chair an extra long time until he "comes down."

The prospect who shows signs of just having come down from his high, will be closely questioned and challenged about this in his interview. The nature of this interrogation, revealing the intimate, inside knowledge of junkies' ways that it does, will help to convince the prospect that he is dealing with a specially qualified group of people and one very different from the conventionally trained professionals with whom he is more familiar.

After the prospect's acceptance into the house he may have to go through withdrawal by "cold turkey" (without medication). How is this managed in Daytop? This question is among those most frequently asked by people who are learning about Daytop for the first time, but in the house itself this is one of the problems that gives least difficulty. It is helpful to compare the situation of the addict withdrawing "cold turkey" in hospital or jail conditions with a similar person undergoing the same thing in Daytop. Here, instead of being put in isolation, attended by staff whose attitude ranges from impersonal and detached to thoroughly hostile, he is in a solidly supportive group of people who have been through the same experience themselves.

"Kicking cold turkey" in Daytop, one is told, is no worse than a bad case of flu. There are several reasons why the agonies of physical withdrawal, as they are manifested in the context of hospital or prison, are so much diminished in Daytop. One is that instead of being in isolation with nothing to do except dwell upon his physical pains, the Daytop resident is part of a lively social group. He can sit with others and play cards, listen to music, talk, and do some light work such as dusting.

In the second place, there is no reward for exaggerating his pains in Daytop as there may be in a hospital where it may earn him some medication. On the contrary, any attempt by the new resident in Daytop to over-dramatize his withdrawal problems will be met at first with humorous ridicule and, if he persists, with sterner "put downs." So long as he "grins and bears it" he is rewarded by the attention and concern of his peers, who accept him as a member of the group and offer help in practical ways such as massaging his back or taking him to the showers.

A third point, which we have touched on already, is the fact that the person undergoing withdrawal in Daytop is interacting with others who have been through the same experience themselves. This means that they can identify with what he is experiencing and that he can tell they do. This sharing of the experience lessens its wretchedness. We see here an interesting example of the way in which physical symptoms can be radically affected by the social context in which the person finds himself.

If the new resident was required to have a haircut as part of his investment this will have been done before he is taken around for his introductions. He will also have given up his jewelry and other personal possessions, as well as any ostentatious clothing that he may have been wearing.

As a novice or brand-new resident he will probably not be assigned to a room right away but will sleep on a couch in the living room. He is assigned to a work area or department, usually the service crew or kitchen, or in the case of females it may be the housekeeping department.

Novices are strongly discouraged from talking to other novices, lest they reinforce each other's negative attitudes and tend to form a mutually reinforcing group of deviants within the house. New residents who were previously friends before may be "put on a ban" and formally forbidden to socialize with each other at all. It is fundamental to the Daytop social system that all peer groupings in the house should overtly stand for the same values as the house stands for. Those who are not yet ready to make a full commitment to Daytop values must not be allowed to form deviant groups which would hold them back from developing such a commitment. At the same time, the older members are putting themselves out to "pull in" the newcomers, to be friendly to them and acquaint them with the ways of Daytop and to talk over problems. Senior members are supposed to keep an eye on the novices to see that they are not neglected, not withdrawing (for example, behind books or into watching T.V.) or that they are not getting depressed. If need be, they will go and chat with them or will tell some other residents who have been around a few months to do so.

Gradually the novice is drawn into the various facets of the communal life of Daytop. He will have his first work assignment, which is invariably menial. He will be introduced to the encounter groups and to the "seminars" (discussions and public speaking groups). His head of department will make a formal "attitude report" on his conduct at the end of each week. He may figure occasionally in the daily discussion of residents' progress held by directors and coordinators.

As time goes by, the new resident will not find it easy to live up to Daytop standards. He will get reprimands and get into trouble sometimes but he will also make some progress. His roommates will be changed periodically so that he is forced to get to know more of the residents. His jobs will be changed so that he has to learn how to cope with new kinds of problems. In encounters he will find himself pushed into participating more. As he progresses, he moves to more responsible statuses within the house. Soon he himself is helping to induct new entrants. Life now has hope and meaning for him but is far from being easy. The policy of the house keeps him moving to new stress situations periodically.

No two people have the same problem areas but certain ones come up again and again: giving orders, taking orders, making pull-ups, discussing feelings, relating to the opposite sex, speaking in public, doing certain kinds of jobs. Daytop policy is to move people around to different jobs quite frequently so as to expose them to a great range of different situations. They stay in each position until it ceases to be a challenge, then when it begins to become easy they are moved. In this way all are forced to learn how to deal with their problem areas instead of avoiding them. That is, they are forced to learn—unless they "split."

Daytop is not primarily a supportive environment but a therapeutic one. The aim is not just to help the resident to live with his problem by providing an organized peer group as a crutch while leaving the real personality problem untouched. Rather Daytop's aim is to cure his problem, to help him change as a person using the whole therapeutic environment as a "pressure cooker" to bring about perhaps ten normal years of character development within two years. Daytop offers not crutches but major surgery—and basically, a do-it-yourself form of surgery.

The usual attitudes to the addict, either punishing him for his addiction or pitying him for it and babying him, are rejected in Daytop as having no therapeutic value, that is, no potential to help the addict change and give up his dependence. On the contrary, they both tend to reinforce the addict in his behavior. What he will get here is "reality therapy," forcing him to look objectively at how he acts and the consequences of his actions, and demanding that he change behavior that does not conform to the Daytop Concept.

This treatment begins with the dramatized dressing down, which the "prospect" (applicant for membership) receives in his initial interview. Its function is to shock him into loosening his grip on his old defense mechanisms. This approach works as well as it does because the people who tell him these mortifying truths about himself are themselves former addicts. He cannot shrug them off as being squares who have no understanding of what it feels like from his side. They do know and they have themselves been through the treatment they are putting him through. This is perhaps the greatest advantage which the community of ex-addicts has over any institution or program run by "them" (the staff) for "us" (the patients).

The newcomer sees Daytop as an established and ongoing community. Residents are at all stages of progress, from recent entries to members of two years or more who have jobs on the outside or top-level positions in the Daytop hierarchy. Older residents have a strong sense of loyalty to the Daytop community, realizing that through it they have begun to find a happier life. Those residents stand as "positive role models" and living examples to the newcomers that addicts can kick the habit and change their outlook. They will encourage and pressure the newcomers to conform to the rules and expectations of their community or, as they often call it, "our family."

No hospital, conventional "treatment program," and certainly no prison can give the addict who has just rolled in off the street these positive role models. In prison or hospital those who set the tone for the other inmates are those who act craziest or toughest, the ones with the biggest habit, the ones with the best "hustles" or confidence rackets. In Daytop, by contrast, the tone is set by the residents with the most responsible attitudes. Those who are not prepared to strive to become more responsible, more considerate and to be more honest with themselves do not stay.

Whereas attendance in hospital or prison is a penalty, being in Daytop is a privilege that has to be earned by making an initial investment and by continued effort. Residents are sometimes thrown out. The fact that Daytop can be selective in whom it takes and whom it keeps is crucial to maintaining a high degree of at least outward compliance among the established members. This, in turn, is essential to its success as an ongoing community and to its success in bringing about attitude changes in its members.

BASIC NORMS AND RULES

Neither the new resident nor the researcher finds any difficulty at all in getting to know the basic norms and rules of Daytop, since they are constantly being expounded in a highly explicit fashion. This is readily understandable in view of the fact that new members are continually being accepted and must be socialized into an understanding of and compliance with the norms of this group. Furthermore, this socialization process is attempted over a short period of time (the total length of time spent in Daytop by those who stay to complete the course is only about two years and out of this time only a fraction is mainly devoted to learning to comply with the ground rules of the community). It must also be remembered that drug addicts are noted, above all, for their unwillingness to conform to the norms of conventional society, and only in the most attenuated sense could they be considered conformists to a subculture of their own. Given the problem Daytop must solve in order to survive—that of socializing a constant stream of new members, recruited from the most asocial section of society, in a short space of time—it is not hard to see why the norms and rules of this group are very explicitly stated. The value system which underlies these norms and rules is clearly seen to be an antidrug, anticrime value system. It represents a complete reversal of the values lived by the junkie. This too is emphasized quite explicitly. The Daytop way of life is the complete antithesis of the junkie subculture of "the streets." This radical reversal in values and way of life also implies a very explicit and unequivocal way of stating the new norms and rules.

To maintain conformity to such a normative system requires, of course, more than just the clear and explicit articulation of the expectations themselves. It also requires a system for monitoring effectively the behavior of group members and a system of sanctions for reinforcing conformity and deterring deviance. We shall discuss the monitoring systems and the elaborate system of sanctions which exists in Daytop in a later chapter. In this chapter our purpose is to outline the main features of the Daytop normative system. As indicated, the verbal articulation of group norms, in informal and formal situations, in one-to-one conversations and in group meetings, is very much part of "the Daytop Concept." *Teaching* new residents the rules of the house and *reinforcing* particular rules which are being overlooked are themselves expected forms of behavior.

"Pulling in" new residents, as it is termed, is recognized as a highly important duty that older and middle-level residents should be attending to. They are frequently reminded to make more effort at this and reminded, "Where would we be if the older people hadn't pulled us in when we were new in the house? We'd be back out there shooting dope and killing ourselves." But "pulling in the new brothers and sisters" is not merely for the purpose of helping them to understand the rules and procedures of Daytop, though this is important. Even more important is the latent function of this practice, which is to help the new resident feel that certain people in this place are concerned about him, that they care about him. When questioned about his main impressions of Daytop when he was a new resident (six years prior to the interview), Richie Rode, who became a graduate and then a director, cited this very point.

Q: Can you remember when you were really new in the house what your impression—your feeling about the place was? When you were in only (say) a few weeks?

A: Well, my impression of it was that the people who were there were really concerned about me. And people were really willing to take out a lot of time—time and effort to really sit down with you and explain things to you. I was really pulled in well. People would really take the time to make sure that you understood what was going on. And even when I was a new resident and I got into trouble, you know, I always felt the concern, along with whatever I was being reprimanded for.

Thus one of the basic norms is to lend one's voice to teaching new residents about the norms of the house and emphasizing their importance in group situations. Because of the existence of this norm, the task of the investigator is relatively easy in this area. Merely by residing in the house for a few days and keeping one's ears open one is bound to learn most of the more salient rules. By asking a few questions most of the gaps will be filled in quite willingly.

The "cardinal rules" of Daytop forbid the use of any drugs and the use of violence. These rules are considered extremely important; violations are considered "hanging offenses" and may lead to the most severe consequences, quite possibly expulsion from the house. The "no drugs" rule covers the unauthorized use of any chemicals, including alcohol. No "chemical highs" are allowed, though social drinking is permitted for residents who are in the last stages before graduating. "Drinking privileges" are awarded to each such resident individually, when senior staff think fit. Any medication which a resident may have been prescribed by a physician while in Daytop is kept under lock and key in the medical department and is issued to him one dose at a time. Even aspirin is regulated in this rigorous way.

The taboo against violence is mentioned far more often than the taboo against drugs. This is not because it is more important but because the taboo against drugs is all too obvious and also because the temptations to succumb to the use of violence present themselves far more often and far more readily to Daytop residents. They will not very often get the chance to abuse some drug, precisely because such great care is taken to remove them from the reach of residents. Every new resident entering the house is meticulously searched for contraband drugs by former junkies who know all the bodily orifices which can conceal such contraband and all visitors to the house are carefully screened and watched. But many times each day residents must be tempted to strike out against someone out of the frustrations and aggravations of living in a community so strictly regulated as this, where they are required to follow orders meekly, without complaint, and listen to scathing public denunciations of their shortcomings.

It is explained that everyone who is here in Daytop is here in order to learn how to deal with stress, frustration, and anger in a mature and adult way, instead of always acting out their feelings (for example, by hitting out at the person who has angered one) or by running away from the difficult situation (for example, by the use of drugs). In the culture of the street-junkie, violence is often used in order to get one's own way, regardless of the rights and wrongs involved in the dispute. For this reason, too, violence is tabooed in Daytop. In order for people to learn more mature patterns of behavior, drugs (escaping from the problem) and violence (childishness, impulsiveness, and unreasonable attempts to impose one's own will) must be ruled out. As a house director said one time in morning meeting, "Here you don't show you're a man by fighting or by taking a beating for what you believe in, like it was on the street. Here you show you're a man by your openness and honesty."

In fact, violations of these two cardinal rules are exceedingly rare. Examining the daily logs kept from almost the beginning of Daytop up till 1968 revealed only one recorded instance of actual violence, which led to the expulsion of the offender. In the early months of Daytop Lodge, when a series of ineffective directors were in charge, drugs were being smuggled freely into the house and used there. Since the arrival of David Deitch, though, Daytop has been a drug-free group and one in which a high level of conformity to its social norms is maintained. We continue our outline of those norms.

In addition to the two cardinal rules, there are others which are also very important. The orders of house directors and other residents in positions of delegated authority must be obeyed without protest. "Reacting" to directions, that is to say protesting, complaining, or following the order in a disrespectful manner, is forbidden and when it happens is sternly dealt with. Any grievances which residents may have, arising from orders which they consider unreasonable, discriminatory, or offensive, may be vented in encounter groups but residents must control their feelings of grievance at the time. To be more precise, they must not act out their annoyance; they must not give way to impulses but must control them like an adult. They are entitled to anger and feelings of grievance, but must save the expression of them for the appropriate time and place, which in Daytop is the encounter group.

Daytop residents are expected to work hard at their assigned tasks and to take pride in their work. They are not allowed to take anything which does not belong to them without asking permission—whether it is food from the kitchen, a pencil from an office, or a cigarette from someone else's pack. Taking something without permission is regarded as "stealing" and is dealt with sternly. Residents are told not to make assumptions but, when in doubt about anything in Daytop, to ask. The existence of this rule removes a great many possible excuses for misconduct. Along with this rule is the related one that all residents are expected to go out of their way to "pull in our younger brothers and sisters," that is to explain to them how things are done in Daytop. This requires not just a willingness to answer their questions, but taking the initiative themselves, to explain Daytop rules and procedures along with the reasons given for their existence.

This is part of a wider Daytop norm of concern for other members, which is one of the most fundamental norms in Daytop. In contrast with the cardinal rules forbidding the use of drugs or violence, this norm states what residents *should* do. Frequent reference is made to the norm of concern in the daily routine at Daytop. For example, the following situations were observed.

> In morning meeting Louise mentions that Benny, a new resident, missed a discussion group which he was supposed to attend because he did not even know that such a group existed, let alone that he was supposed to attend one.
>
> "How long is he in the house?"
>
> "I think we should all look at that. Why aren't we teaching our new brothers?"

This is a straightforward reference to a well-understood norm. A second example reveals the existence of this same norm less directly.

> One night the writer, as participant observer, is working late in the Daytop Communications Office. Mike (an expediter and resident of some six months standing) looks into the office in the course of his rounds. He tells me that I should not work so late, that I should take some time to relax and get to know the other residents. He also upbraids Bobby, who is working in the office with me, for not pointing this out to me, in other words for not showing enough concern for a newer member of the group.

A third example illustrating the Daytop norm of having concern for others is the following:

> Juanita comes into the living room and asks for everyone's attention. Everyone stops talking and looks to see what she wants. Work time is over and most residents are relaxing or doing odd jobs. She says that she has some work to do down in the laundry room and, as no one else is down there, she will be lonely. Will one of her "family" please come to keep her company? Someone offers to do so. He is showing some concern—though the purity of his concern is possibly questionable, since she is an attractive girl. And arguably it is no sacrifice for him to keep her company for half an hour or so. There is, however, another actor in this little playlet who is showing concern of a rather refined kind. This is Charlie, who tells me proudly that Juanita had asked him to accompany her but he had another commitment. What he did do, though, is that he persuaded her (against her timid inclinations) to make her announcement in the way she did, as a result of which she not only got some company but approval for the way in which she went about it and good feelings for having overcome her fears of making the announcement. The announcement is clearly an appeal to an accepted group norm of concern for each other and Charlie's pleasure in telling how he encouraged her to overcome her fears of making the announcement clearly reflects his feeling that in doing this he was living up to the norm of concern in a rather sophisticated way.

The kind of concern which Daytop residents are supposed to show towards each other is defined as "responsible" concern. A distinction is drawn between doing what the other person wants and doing what is good for them. Responsible concern is doing what is good for them, like the parent who refuses to give a child something dangerous which he wants to play with. Thus it is responsible concern to point out a person's mistake in front of others, when it is embarrassing to the person who made the mistake, because the embarrassment will help them learn not to make that mistake again. This is Daytop policy, justified on the grounds that experience has shown it to be the only way to change the behavior of junkies or "people like us."

> Two or three residents may be sitting together talking and drinking coffee. One of them gets up and leaves, forgetting to clear away his dirty cup. By the norms of the outside community, one would be expected to pick up the cup for him, without comment. In Daytop, though, this would be regarded as a lamentable failure to show responsible concern to the forgetful person and help him to be more aware in the future by calling it to his attention, quite forcefully, in front of others.

Another aspect of the responsible concern ethic is a strict honor code which repudiates the "no squealing" rule of the streets. If a fellow resident in Daytop shares a guilty secret with you, you are required and expected to report this to a senior member. Failure to do this, if it later comes to light, is severely dealt with. The reason for such sternness is not just that the authority of the house is being violated by breaking a rule, but also that the resident who helps his fellow conceal the guilty secret is acting against the true interests of his fellow, which require him (like everyone else in Daytop) to be completely open with *all* his peers in the Daytop group. The rule of "no secrets" and no "negative contracts" (private agreements to violate the rules of Daytop) is justified on the grounds that, in order to make the kinds of radical change in one's attitudes and behavior that everyone in Daytop is supposedly trying to make, it is necessary for each one to be completely open and honest with his fellows in the therapeutic community. It is necessary to keep secrets from one's fellows only if one is trying to maintain self-deceptions; openness and honesty with "the family" enables them to help one break down such harmful illusions. Thus a responsible concern for one's peers in Daytop requires that any attempt they may make to set up a negative contract involving shared secrets should be exposed—for the good of the other person—even though he is "getting into trouble" as a result of the exposure.

Honesty is a fundamental value in Daytop. So is "openness." One is expected to tell the truth and the *whole* truth. "Confronting" and being confronted are central concepts in the Daytop way of life. Daytop residents are supposed to confront each other frequently. If you suspect that a fellow resident is worried or "uptight", if you suspect that he is thinking of doing something foolish or that he has already done it, it is your duty to confront him with your suspicions. If you feel uncomfortable with a certain person, you are expected to mention this to him ("confront" him about it)—whether you think you know the reason for this or not. Then the two of you can talk about it and possibly get to the bottom of the matter and improve things; and even if you fail to resolve it, the mere fact of having brought the difficulty out into the open is expected to improve the situation somewhat—at least subjectively, in the sense that you will feel better about it.

Confronting the person who seems to be uptight about something may help him to talk about what is bothering him and to do something about the underlying problem. This is clearly an instance of responsible concern. Confronting the person whom you suspect of hiding some guilty secret will, if your suspicions are well founded, arouse his guilt feelings and make it harder for him to continue to conceal it.

Honesty and confrontation are connected to the norm of "relating." Residents are supposed to "relate" to each other at all times, except when they are hard at work; that is, to talk about themselves, how they are feeling, what has happened lately to make them feel good or bad, what they are learning about themselves and so forth. The norm of relating requires each resident to spend some time in relating to *all* the other members of the house. The formation of exclusive cliques is expressly forbidden, though it is recognized that some individuals will form specially close relationships. Most times when residents are neither working nor sleeping they are supposed to be "on the floor," that is, in the living room or the dining room on the main floor. It is forbidden to "isolate" oneself or for small groups to get together away from the main areas where residents gather—unless they are accompanied by a senior resident. Isolated individuals are not relating and small groups which are away from the surveillance of senior members of the house may easily lapse into "negative" talk (talking about their old way of life in a nostalgic vein or criticizing Daytop rules). Any time a resident leaves the building (even to go out in the grounds) he is required to check out, by placing a colored tag against his name on a board at the front desk, and upon returning to remove it. This enables the whereabouts of every resident to be known approximately at all times. It also serves to keep residents "aware" and to remind them that they are in Daytop and under various restrictions.

In the area of work there is the strong emphasis on "quality," a perfectionism which involves frequent inspection of one's work by the department head or coordinator who will have no hesitation in ordering a whole job to be redone if he is dissatisfied with some small part of it. Thus, for example, a whole floor may have to be repolished, or a whole letter retyped on account of a single flaw.

Special rules apply to relationships between males and females in Daytop. The basic idea is for residents to treat one another as brothers and sisters of a large family. The rules about relating and being open and honest apply equally between the sexes. An emphasis is laid on relating to people as people without regard to difference of sex—or the other differences of age, race, education, and so forth which commonly structure the way people treat each other. Just as it is forbidden to "act out" with violence or drugs, it is also forbidden for residents to engage in any sexual activities. Flirting between residents is forbidden and precautionary rules exist to help prevent it.

> One evening the writer and two female residents were about to go out into the grounds for a walk. One of the girls was called away to take care of some unfinished job and the other one indicated to me that we must stay in sight of the house when we went out into the grounds, since we were now an unchaperoned male-female pair.

This is a formidable body of norms—and obviously an account such as this is incomplete and can only outline the more important ones. These norms prescribe a way of life radically different from that formerly lived by Daytop residents. Hence there has to be intensive teaching and socialization of new members and, in addition, a system of social controls to maintain the high level of conformity which is found in Daytop. The culture of this unusual group is a highly self-conscious and "rational" one. It is rational in the sense that reasons are readily provided for just about every norm and regulation. These reasons always lead back to the central premise that Daytop is a group of people with a common problem—the need to break away from a former pattern of life which has brought them misery and trouble. This can only be achieved by strenuous efforts on their own behalf, with the help of each other, following the guidelines of the Daytop Concept. Others have walked this path and shown that it does indeed lead to being able to stand on one's own feet, to be able to live without drugs, as a responsible and self-respecting adult. Some of these graduates, who validate the system, are in staff positions at Daytop at the present, living proof of the efficacy of the Daytop Concept.

MOTIVATION

The standards of conduct demanded of residents in Daytop are high and high levels of conformity to these standards are demanded. At the same time, however, we must remember that the Daytop Concept emphasizes fraternalism and mutual help and concern. Most of the normative demands can thus be seen as creating the necessary conditions for a warm, fraternal group. So the reward for conformity is, not just to avoid the negative sanctions that are applied to deviants, but also partly to enjoy the warm and secure feeling of belonging to this close-knit group. There is, too, the feeling of personal satisfaction of knowing one is succeeding at doing things that previously seemed too difficult to consider. The specific achievements will be different with different individuals: for some it may be doing a job well, for others speaking up in front of people, or even just getting up on time in the morning and making one's own bed. The other part of the reward for conformity is finding for the first time that one can feel really close to certain individuals, feel concern from them and feel concern for them, trust them, and feel good about experiencing all of these feelings. These are the really significant dimensions of personal growth in Daytop—gingerly unfolding the tightly closed petals of one's innermost feelings, to make contact on a human level. One learns to relate to other people in terms of the common, human emotions that both share—fears, hopes, shame, pride, love—rather than just in terms of the superficial factors that have determined and limited their relationships previously. In Daytop, people learn to relate to each other as *people,* despite superficial differences of age, sex, ethnic background, race, education, social class, and so forth. The population in Daytop is in fact an extremely heterogeneous one in terms of all these variables and members of these different groups live in harmony together.

In trying to understand the achievement of Daytop we have to keep in mind the kind of person the narcotic addict is when living outside such a therapeutic community. We shall review several psychiatric and psychological studies of the narcotic addict and then add a summary of the testimony of Daytop people about themselves as they used to be. Both sources are subject to serious but unmeasurable biases. Daytop residents' self-descriptions may be regarded as biased by what they have been taught in Daytop and the "scientific" accounts may be biased by the fact that the addicts studied were already hospitalized. That fact entails a bias of sampling, raising the question of whether these individuals are representative. It also entails a further bias due to the fact that hospitalized addicts have usually been through highly unpleasant experiences prior to and as a result of admission to a hospital. In addition, they are commonly attempting to manipulate staff into giving them drugs. For all these reasons the behavior of addicts in a hospital cannot be assumed to be the same as their behavior outside, though in many respects it probably is. We shall, therefore, combine both sources of information and hope that at least some of the biases inherent in each source will cancel each other out.

There is no one psychiatric diagnostic category into which addicts uniquely fall, but certain characteristics of personality are fairly widely attributed to them. In general at this time it is impossible to separate the psychological traits of the addict *before* his addiction which caused him to be addiction-prone from other traits brought on as a *result* of the addiction. Here, then, are several quotations from the literature on the typical personality of the addict.

> Almost all heroin addicts are childishly immature; full of demands, empty of offerings. When they want something, they want it yesterday and they want it effortlessly. Nothing is their fault—their addiction, their degradation, their desperation. All are insecure, most dislike people, and—though the mechanics of obtaining and injecting drugs forces them into relationships with other people—most would prefer to be alone. . . None can tolerate "changes" . . . most of them are extremely narcissistic. . . Perhaps the dominant emotional characteristic of the addict is his enormous compulsion to abdicate all responsibility for his own life. He craves to be told what to do. (Mills, 1966)

> Addicts tolerate anxiety poorly: they "act out"; they often engage in self-destructive behavior that is not consciously recognized as self-detrimental. Secondly, as Wikler has suggested, addiction, once established is probably affected by unconscious or operant conditioned responses that make the obtaining of drugs a way of life. (Vaillent, 1966)

> They, by and large, have never grown up, distrust everyone in authority (and virtually everybody else) and have substituted drug-taking for practically everything that occupies other people. (National Institute of Mental Health, 1963)

> Juvenile addicts in general—even before they take drugs—are easily frustrated and made anxious, and they find both states intolerable. They cannot enter into prolonged, close, friendly relations with others; they have difficulties assuming a masculine role. (*Ibid.*)

> In most instances the addict's sins are those of omission rather than commission; they are ineffective people, individuals whose great desire is to withdraw from the world and its troubles into a land of dreams. (Joint Committee of AMA and ABA, 1960)

> Entrance into addiction has the significance of elevation to a ceremonial group association. Addicts speak almost a separate language . . . there is a considerable sense of "belonging," and this is not easily given up unless some new group appeal takes its place. . . The typical heroin addict has likewise usually described a profound sense of loneliness and isolation which partly disappeared on his entering the separate world of addiction. (Fort, 1966)

Daytop residents agree with these experts on several points: on their own intolerance of stress, impulsiveness, lack of control, tendency to whine about problems or run away from them rather than work constructively to improve the situation, their loneliness, lack of strong ties of friendship, distrustfulness, and feelings of inadequacy. This last factor is emphasized a lot more in Daytop than it is in the published literature. "Feeling bad about yourself," "poor self-image" or whatever name is given to it, is seen to lie at the heart of the addict's problem and to be one of the main keys in his task of changing himself. Other attributes of the addict mentioned in Daytop but not encountered in the literature are: feeling like a loser, feeling paranoid, feeling unique, and believing that no one else could understand his problems.

These, then, are the kinds of people we find in Daytop. These are the kinds of problems they are struggling against. As we examine the different facets of the Daytop way of life it will be important to keep in mind these personality characteristics and to consider how the different features of the Daytop way of life either fit this kind of person or how they help to make him change in the direction necessary to be able to live without depending on drugs. For example, the communal aspect of Daytop life appeals to the addict's loneliness and need to feel that he belongs to a group while the prohibition against "reacting" to another person by any incivility forces him to learn to control his impulsiveness.

In Daytop the addict (or "*former* addict" as they insist on being called, with staff encouragement) lives in a precarious state of balance, poised between the pull of two sets of forces: the positive forces pulling him to stay in Daytop and make the most of himself as a human being, and the negative forces pulling him to give that up and return to the old life of having fun, getting "high," not having to worry about getting into trouble with his Daytop bosses for mistakes which would be considered trivial outside. Of course, returning to the outside society also entails all the hassles of getting enough money to buy dope, risking arrest, and being robbed by other addicts, but when the former addict is feeling nostalgic or when things have been difficult for him in Daytop he is inclined to forget these aspects of life on the street. For this reason residents are constantly reminded that whenever they feel uptight they should ask to sit down and talk with someone. They will then find that someone else can understand and identify with their feelings of wanting to "split" from the house, for every resident does feel this way at times, and they can then both talk more realistically about the outside world and the reasons for staying in Daytop. Even more than the reasons which they review, the manifest concern shown in that situation helps the resident who is getting restless to decide to stay, though not always, of course. Many do leave anyway and some regret their decision and seek to return.

One of the biggest problems Daytop has, is to deal with the problem of residents wanting to split and then wanting to come back. It is, of course, intimately related to the kind of person the addict is—especially to his impulsiveness and fickleness. The Daytop rule is that a resident who still wants to split after he has talked with someone must sit on the prospect chair. After he has been left there for a while to think over his decision in a chilling isolation, he is then brought back for a further talk. If he still wants to split, he will be given bus fare, his personal possessions which he initially brought into the house with him and he will be escorted to the bus.

The splittee who wants to get back into the house must go through an even more severe version of the admission procedure that he initially experienced. Instead of facing just a small group of interviewers, the splittee usually has to face a general meeting of the whole house. They will challenge him about what he did while out of the house and express their feelings about his having rejected them in no uncertain terms. Especially individuals with whom he was at all close before he split will let him know quite vehemently how much he hurt them by splitting. Splittees who did not even have the decency to go about leaving in the right way but who sneaked out of the house secretly without telling anyone are the object of much verbal hostility.

The fact is that each person who splits from Daytop is a potential threat to the motivation of every other resident since he stirs up their latent desires to give up the struggle. For everyone's sake, including that of the prospective splittee himself, everything possible must be done to discourage him from splitting. Letting everyone see earlier splittees sitting for very long periods (ten to twenty-four hours) on the prospect chair—the length of time depending on whether they left in the right way or not—is designed to discourage those presently in the house from such thoughts and especially to discourage them from thoughts of splitting "out the back door." A resident who plans to split secretly cannot, of course, be talked to. The fact that residents are not allowed to have any money until they have demonstrated some degree of maturity together with the fact that the Staten Island house is some distance from Manhatten and Brooklyn (the home boroughs of most residents) makes it more worth the splittee's while to talk to someone—just in order to get his bus fare.

What keeps a resident in Daytop? That is a hard question to answer but several factors may be suggested. One is a rational awareness that returning to the outside means putting himself in real jeopardy. As Felix Donawa, a one-time staff member at Daytop, recalls several years after,

> I think the reason I decided to give this Concept a chance was I was really starting to get scared about going to jail. It seemed like in the last two or three years I seemed to be getting arrested like every 90 days and doing like 90 days or 6 months (in jail). Two or three times a year I was getting arrested. Maybe the first two years or so it was all misdemeanors, but now that I had a felony conviction which means that each succeeding time that I would get arrested I would get more time. You know the penalties become that much stiffer. So I think that realizing that I just had a 5 year sentence. Now if I leave and get arrested I owe this 5 years and whatever else I'm gonna do. The time is going to get bigger.

This rational calculation of the risks outside is not enough by itself, though. He must also believe that Daytop can help him change and that he can make it there. Felix goes on to say,

> I know that for me it was one of the main reasons I decided to give it a chance —along with the fact that I felt some of the guys that had been around 6, 7, 8 months seemed sincere and I thought if they can change and this Concept can help them, being how we're from the same background; if I try and apply myself maybe it'll help. I went along on that basis for the longest time until I really felt that I was changing and there were certain advantages to completing the Concept.

At the time of wanting to split residents do not always look at the situation so rationally, of course. Felix never split. The problem, from the standpoint of Daytop staff, is to stall the would-be splittee long enough to make him look rationally at the choice before him. And whether he can be stalled or shoots right out of the door when no one is looking depends to a great extent on two factors: (1) whether anyone is sufficiently aware that he is uptight to confront him and ask him to talk about what is bothering him, or (2) whether he himself feels enough trust and confidence in at least one fellow-resident who happens to be around at the critical time and asks to talk with him. Richie Rode recalls,

> I remember one time I was underneath a car, adjusting the brakes. I was laying there and it was cold and I'm saying "what the fuck am I doing here?" and I said "fuck this." I walked in the house. I talked to my coordinator and told him I felt like splitting. We sat down and talked for about half an hour. Then I didn't feel like splitting anymore. I'd got it out of my system—whatever it was. I just walked outside and got to work.

Closely related to these factors is a third one, that really underlies both the others. It is the development of attachments between the new resident and some other members of the group—attachments in the sense that he likes and respects this other member or members and starts to feel that he does not want to look bad in that person's eyes or to let him down. Richie Rode continues to explain this:

> That's why it's important for the new kid to be pulled in properly. He has to be spoken to. He has to have a feeling that he wants to stay around because he doesn't want to look bad in somebody's eyes that he really respects. Sometimes he doesn't know why he's doing it. But sometimes it's because of this person who pulled him in. He feels "I really like this guy," for the first time in my life. Sometimes when he feels like splitting it's usually those experiences that will keep him around. His so-called "bank of positive experiences" has started to build up already. Otherwise the only way he has of dealing with it is to act off the feeling and go.
>
> Q: Are you looking mainly forwards or backwards?
>
> I think you're also looking ahead. "Well, if I split I'm not going to experience this anymore and it's good."

Jim Germano was one of the earliest residents accepted into Daytop. He had known David Deitch in Synanon, where he (Germano) had spent a year before he split. At Daytop he started at the bottom, though he rose quite rapidly and eventually became Assistant Executive Director, before he left to start his own program, Marathon House in Rhode Island. His explanation of how the drug addict right off the street is turned into a conforming member of a therapeutic community again emphasizes the importance of forming some special attachments, as well as the influence of the normative pressure of the group as a whole.

> What happened with me was that I realized that I was going to remain ostracized, with very little status and recognized as "the village fuck-up" unless I did what was suggested of people there. They're pretty smart people, the people that run these programs. They use the psychology that you shoot dope with to get you to stop shooting dope. Everyone is interested in having the people around them like them and admire them and all this kind of stuff. Out on the street you can do that with a group of junkies and the only criteria for acceptance is how crazy you are—the crazier you are the more pats on the back you get. They throw you into a completely different kind of environment. The people have shared similar experiences but their current behavior, their current attitude seems to be a lot different. In order to gain acceptance and the admiration of the group around you, you have to be a much more "positive" guy. So it takes maybe a month or two to realize that and then a person makes his judgment—whether he figures he can go along with the program.

For him the "special attachment" was with his director, Deitch, so he generalizes or overgeneralizes this to all residents. Undoubtedly, though, for some other residents their special attachment is with some other older resident. We can, however, take his account of how this operates and apply it to those cases too.

> I think in the beginning the relationship you develop with your director is like what psychiatrists call a transference, where you really look to the director like a father figure. You anxiously await his approval for things and it's most painful to get a haircut from him when you're in a position to be reprimanded. Being

> the role model yourself, that is a little bit more abstract and less intense than your relationship with the people that you pick out as *your* role models. You give some thought to your own responsibility as a role model—at least I have but I think that at that time my major motivation was to win approval and pats on the back from Deitch and his wife, Susan. Not the assistant director. I didn't get along with him too well.

Shifting the focus to a later time when the resident is being given positions of some importance in the house, then he starts to develop a new kind of motivation based on defining himself as a role model to newer residents and hence having a responsibility to them as well as to the staff who are depending on him. Jim Germano continues:

> I think when it gets to the point when he's helping to run the place, when he has status and some freedom and he's a *trusted* member of the community, then . . . he really . . . thinks more and more in terms of not letting people down. They're expecting certain things of me. Let me not let anyone down. Let me do what I'm supposed to do.

We have looked at the motivational factors which determine whether or not a resident will stay in spite of the difficult experiences that lie in store for him. We also looked at the process of "pulling in" the new resident and at the development of different levels of motivation to keep him from splitting, if it is done well and if the new person is responsive to it. We must keep in mind, though, the fact that around one quarter of new residents do not last thirty days and another quarter split at some time between the second and the eighteenth month. Thus when we talk about what keeps a person in Daytop we are not talking about a process that always works but one that is nevertheless remarkably effective—considering the kind of people they are dealing with.

3/The framework of organization

In any week several new residents may be accepted into Daytop Village, Staten Island. In any week two or three may split. But the daily and weekly cycle of events continues without interruption. The same rules are taught and enforced, the same values are promulgated by example and explicit teaching. Every weekday begins with morning meeting after breakfast, following a set pattern. Then all residents work in their respective departments until lunch, after which there is seminar. Work is resumed after seminar until supper time and may continue for a while after supper. Three nights each week (Monday, Wednesday, and Friday) encounter groups are held. Such is the daily cycle Monday through Friday.

On Saturday evening Open House is held for the public and the preceding part of the day is mostly spent in preparing for it. Sunday is a "loose day." Such is the weekly cycle. A winter-to-summer cyclical variation is introduced by the weather, which permits little outdoor activities in the winter (due to the cold and snow) and which in the summer is so hot and humid as to make a full day's work very hard some days. As a result of this, work may be canceled for the afternoon on exceptionally hot days in favor of outdoor sports or relaxation. A retreat at the end of the summer brings the residents of both houses together for approximately ten days, at the upstate New York facility in Swan Lake.

New residents are admitted at any time according to the pressure of demand and the availability of space; they are not accepted all on one day, though, as in the public schools. Similarly there is no set time for the official completion of the program or "confirmation," as it is called. Thus mass arrivals and departures do not themselves constitute cyclical features of organizational life, as happens in other "people-processing organizations."

In some respects Daytop fits Goffman's model of a "total institution" (Erving Goffman, 1961; Wheeler, 1966). Residents have no right to privacy; activities are regimented, in the sense that everyone does certain things together at the same time and only at that time.

In one vital respect Daytop does not conform to Goffman's model of the total institution, though. He describes the staff and nonstaff as living in two totally separate worlds. While it is true that in Daytop the staff has enormous power over residents, as well as many privileges which the latter do not enjoy, they are not set apart from them by uniforms or badges, nor by differences in their origins and future prospects. In Daytop all members of staff have been where residents are now; they have all been through the same experiences as low-status residents in the house and through similar experiences on the street. Contrary to Goffman's model, residents can look forward to the possibility of becoming staff members themselves. Thus Daytop is quite unlike total institutions such as the prison or hospital, but there is some similarity to many religious orders which do allow internal mobility.

We shall now examine more closely some of the institutionalized routines of life in Daytop: morning meeting, work, seminar, and Open House.

MORNING MEETING

The first important event of the day in Daytop everyday except Sunday is morning meeting. This takes place promptly at 9 A.M. and attendance is compulsory for all residents. In the summer of 1967 morning meeting was preceded by an announcement over the public address system, "It is now ten minutes to morning meeting." And then later, "It is now morning meeting time." A year later, however, this practice had been discontinued on the grounds that residents should learn to be responsible enough to watch the time for themselves. By this time residents must have completed their toilet, cleaned and tidied their room (or that part of it for which they are personally responsible), and presented themselves looking clean and tidy—though they will be wearing their working clothes ready to start work immediately after the end of morning meeting. The kitchen crew finishes serving breakfast at 8:30 A.M. so that those who wish to eat must appear by that time.

Residents assemble in good time, tightly packing the living room. The sofas and armchairs which belong there are turned to face one way and residents who do not find seats on them bring folding chairs from outside. While waiting for the meeting to start, there is quiet chatting and joking. The atmosphere just before morning meeting is respectful but not solemn. Residents socialize and, sometimes someone will informally organize some group singing.

Promptly at 9 A.M. or within a few minutes thereafter the person conducting morning meeting, recognizable from the fact that he carries the customary clipboard, enters and a hush quickly falls on the gathering. This person is usually a coordinator, or a senior resident who is "assuming" the position of coordinator by assisting and learning the job in preparation for the promotion he seeks.

The first part of morning meeting is routine and unvarying.

"Good morning, family," says the person presiding.

"Good morning, John," everyone replies in unison. (Or, "Good morning, Mary.")

"How does everyone feel this morning?" The leader may ask and then make some joking remark before passing on to the first major and unvarying feature of morning meeting.

"Who wants to read the Philosophy?"

Many hands shoot up, and he chooses someone. The one chosen walks to the front of the room. The person in charge hands him the official copy of the Daytop Philosophy or credo. Before reading it he says, "Good morning, Family," and all reply, "Good morning, Bob."

The Philosophy, written by an earlier resident states:

> We are here because there is no refuge, finally from ourselves. Until a man confronts himself in the eyes and hearts of his fellows, he is running. Until he suffers them to share his secret, he has no safety from it. Afraid to be known, he can know neither himself nor any other. He will be alone.
>
> Where else but in our common ground can we find such a mirror? Here, together, a man can at last appear clearly to himself, not as the giant of his dreams or the dwarf of his fears, but as a man, part of a whole with his share in its purposes. In this ground we can each take root and grow, not alone any more, as in death, but alive—a man among men.

During the reading of the Philosophy there is always an awesome, quasi-religious hush and a solemn look on the faces of all present. It is a moving declaration, and it sums up the situation of the typical Daytop resident with poignancy and power.

After the reading of the Philosophy come the formal "pull-ups." We have mentioned in the previous chapter that individual residents are supposed to make pull-ups on their fellow residents for any infractions of the Daytop rules which they observe someone committing, for instance, leaving a dirty coffee cup on a table, failing to tidy up their work area, leaving a light on in a closet, taking something they were not entitled to have, and so forth. This expectation that each resident play an active part in enforcing the rules of the house extends also to situations where someone discovers evidence of a rule having been broken but no culprit immediately obvious. For example, a dirty coffee cup or ashtray is found when one enters the room or a light is found on in an empty closet, and so forth.

In such cases there is an obligation on the resident who discovers such a thing to take steps to discover who is responsible and to make a pull-up on him. In a house with around one hundred residents, however, it will not always be possible to discover the culprit by individual inquiries. In such cases the pull-up is brought to morning meeting by the one who discovers the delinquency.

At the front desk is kept the "pull-up board," on which he enters his name and a brief summary of the pull-up. This is the same clipboard which the person who runs morning meeting brings in with him. After the reading of the Philosophy, he turns to the pull-ups on the board, sometimes commenting on the length of the list—if it is greater than usual.

He calls each name in turn which appears on the pull-up board. That person then stands and delivers his pull-up. For example:

> When I went into the art room just after nine o'clock last night I found a dirty paint brush in the sink. Who left it there?

Let us suppose for the sake of simplicity that someone raises his hand right away. This does in fact happen fairly often—not always, but perhaps with half the pull-ups brought into morning meeting. The person who raises his hand will be admonished in a way that is designed to be embarrassing for him, so that he should effectively learn not to repeat such behavior.

> Those brushes cost money, and they get ruined when people leave them dirty. Besides, I spent half an hour asking around, trying to find out who left that brush

> there. That's a real drag, man. I don't need to waste my time in that way chasing around after dingbats who have no consideration for others. The result was that I had hardly any time to do what I went up there for, and I really don't like it. So get a grip on yourself.

Many pull-ups take this form and are cast in language as least as forceful as this. Other residents raise their hands to be allowed to emphasize or "elaborate" upon the point. The person running morning meeting calls upon whom he wishes. Sometimes he will feel that no further elaboration is necessary if the pull-up has been made forcefully, or he will call upon two or three others to elaborate. When he considers the incident sufficiently important, he will elaborate himself—sometimes at great length.

Elaboration serves various functions. On an immediate level, it emphasizes the rule in the minds of all present and helps them to see why it is important to avoid that kind of behavior. In this way the significance of what seemed to be quite a small incident (such as forgetting to switch off lights or clear away a dirty plate) can be seen in a totally different light—as a symptom or indication of an underlying negative attitude.

The following elaboration was given during a morning meeting at the annual retreat in Swan Lake, upstate New York. Pull-ups had been made about towels and other items which were left by the pool.

> Let's not just think about those towels but think about the *people*. What this means is that people around here are not aware. They are so encapsulated that if there was a pink elephant in this room they wouldn't even see it. And if one of their brothers in the house was uptight and ready to split, they wouldn't notice that either—just like they never noticed that they had left those towels there, and no one noticed that they were lying there until the next day.

One factor determining whether a particular pull-up is reinforced, either by the person running the meeting or by others whom he calls upon, is whether the guilty one is a frequent offender in this respect or not. The example just given represents a pull-up of moderate severity. If a sterner pull-up is felt to be required, the comments just quoted might be followed up by another resident who says,

> When are you going to get a grip on yourself, dummy? You've been in here six weeks and all you do is wander about in a daze, leaving dirty paint brushes behind you, dirty coffee cups, leaving lights on, losing your clothes and I don't know what else. I guess you must sleep in your clothes—otherwise I am sure you'd forget to put them on before you came down in the morning. Get a grip on yourself, stupid.

No one laughs during pull-ups, though there is often considerable humor in the way they are delivered. A pull-up is a serious matter; it is a basic teaching device at Daytop. Not only should the particular culprit be learning from the pull-up, but so should everyone in the meeting. The first function of elaboration is to reinforce and drive home the message of the pull-up. Some elaborations are boring, of course, and some are incomprehensible, but the net effect of this procedure is to define very effectively the socially sanctioned interpretations of behavior in this group. An atmosphere is created in which no resident can *publicly* challenge these interpretations, though one might do so within the confines of the encounter group.

Elaboration has a second and less obvious function. It helps those who do the elaboration to internalize these norms and values. All residents are expected to raise their hands to offer elaborations, though the newer members seldom do this. This willingness to "stand up and be counted" is one criterion which is used to evaluate how hard a resident is trying to "do his thing" in Daytop. And that evaluation determines his rate of promotion and how fast he is allowed his privileges (personal possessions, movie trips, phone calls, letters, etc.). Equally, residents who do not offer to elaborate in morning meeting may be "pointed out" and embarrassed publicly. These are two powerful incentives for those who elaborate in morning meeting.

On those occasions when no one "cops to" the offense (confesses) immediately, further steps are taken and pressure is applied.

One approach is to threaten to institute some kind of inspection which will reveal who is the guilty party. For example, when a razor blade was left in the bathroom, and no one copped to being responsible, simply requiring each male resident to produce his razor blade (only one being issued to each resident in return for his old one) would clearly reveal the culprit. Just the threat of such an inspection will sometimes produce a confession—though sometimes the forgetful one may not even realize that it is he who is guilty of the offense under discussion.

Another approach is to emphasize the importance of honesty and to emphasize that copping to mistakes is taken as a sign of maturity in Daytop. This, set against the embarrassment of the pull-up, is a more subtle incentive.

"How do you feel towards someone who raises his hand and cops to something?" asks the person presiding over the morning meeting one day.

"I look at him like he has something going for him, since he has the heart to raise his hand."

Or, on another occasion a resident volunteered the following statement, designed to encourage a reluctant person to come forward and admit his responsibility for an infraction.

> The question is whether you are man enough to put up your hand and cop to it. Why are people afraid? What makes them hold that guilt in their bellies? What could possibly happen to you for copping to a dirty coffee cup?

On another occasion the person presiding over morning meeting when no one is willing to cop to a pull-up despite several appeals asks, "Who are the newest residents in the House?"

Then he asks them, "How do you feel about this?"

After a pause, Julio says, "It makes me think that this house isn't all you say it is."

> You heard that. You heard what our new brother thinks. He thinks that it's all bullshit what we preach in this house. How can we help them if we don't practice what we preach?

One time when a fairly new resident raised his hand to cop to something, one of his older fellows stood up to praise him for having the good sense to be honest about it. "See, did anything happen to him?"

As a last resort, when all else fails or when for some reason the person in charge does not feel like trying these more gentle approaches, there is the method of repeated guilt arousal. For example, when one of the radios belonging to the house was found smashed and no one copped to being responsible for it, the resident who brought it into morning meeting was told "bring it up tomorrow, Pat, and again and again—until that person can't take the guilt any more." Often when it is announced that this policy is to be followed, someone will follow up with a further appeal to the guilty person to cop to the thing now rather than undergo days or even weeks of misery, racked by guilt feelings every time he sees the broken radio (or whatever the object may be). Residents are also told that many people in this situation before have refused to cop to their guilt and, unable to handle the guilt feelings, they split from Daytop and inevitably turned again to dope. This is sometimes sufficient to scare a confession out of the person concerned—if not immediately in the meeting, then shortly thereafter.

Pull-ups are a major feature of morning meeting, though there is considerable variation in the number of pull-ups and the amount of time devoted to them. There is no necessary correlation between the number of pull-ups and the time taken. Ten pull-ups may be disposed of in ten minutes or may occupy the best part of an hour; a couple of pull-ups may, on the other hand, with all the elaborations, take a full half-hour.

After pull-ups, announcements are made. Some are just routine business, for example, "There will be softball practice after supper tonight," or "men's laundry will be collected on Thursday instead of Friday this week." Other announcements have a real therapeutic importance. They may be apologies to the house which a resident has been told or has been offered to make in order to help to "clean up" something he has done wrong; they may be confessions; they may be appeals for help with a behavioral problem that a resident has to work on. Frequently they are all three together. Here are some actual examples:

> I want to let everyone know why I got this bald head. It was for stealing donuts from the kitchen. That was very stupid of me because I could probably have had them if I had just asked. Would you please help me?
>
> I want to apologize to everyone for breaking my diet.
>
> I want to apologize to everyone for my irresponsible behavior. When I was on a trip to another house I told one of the newer residents that someone had split from our house. She was close with him at one time, and it could have shot her right out of the door.

A resident making this kind of announcement always goes to the front of the room and faces the whole house. It is always a very painful experience for him, and also for others. If he seems to be holding anything back or trying in any way to make his offense seem less serious, he will be sharply corrected. On one occasion someone began an announcement "I took things from the kitchen . . ." He was loudly reminded, "You *stole* them," for this is the way such an offense is regarded in Daytop.

Occasionally someone raises a hand in morning meeting in order to talk about something more pleasant. On one July fifth someone stood up when called upon to speak and said, "I have some good feelings I want to share with everyone." And he went on to describe how good he felt yesterday during the Fourth of July festivities in the house. He thought of previous July Fourths and Christmases and how he had been living then. This was the first time he had ever planned anything special with other people. He felt good that he was doing something worthwhile with his life at last.

We have now entered the second half of morning meeting. This is considerably more lighthearted and jolly than the first half of the meeting, which we have just been describing, in which the serious business takes place. Someone may offer to tell a joke. Someone else stands up to announce the day's menu, spiced with some form of humor, and sometimes sung to a strong beat delivered by eighty or more pairs of clapping hands. Someone else gives a weather report, also packaged with a joke. Someone else reads the current issue of "The Daily Blah," containing humorous accounts of recent events in the house and jokes on some of the personalities in the house. Finally, to end the meeting, one or several residents volunteer (or are press-ganged) into leading the whole house in a rousing song.

The function of the second half of morning meeting is to arouse some group spirit of a lighthearted nature and to send everyone off to work, if possible, in a happy frame of mind—at least, a happier one than they would have had without the second half. Some mornings, when there are serious delinquencies to be dealt with or delinquencies which no one will cop to, the "heavy" first part of morning meeting will take up the greater part of the hour. In the most serious cases, the person running morning meeting will announce that there is no second half to the meeting because the bad attitude of so many people has resulted in no time being left, or simply because the house is not "deserving" today.

The first half of morning meeting is dominated by an earnestness—a sense that serious matters are being dealt with here. The reading of the Philosophy sets a note of solemnity and the elaborations on pull-ups, pointing out the seriousness of apparently trivial delinquencies tends to generate a feeling of moral earnestness. In the second half, though, a spontaneous humor and jocularity comes through. This is apparently enjoyed by most residents. If the second half should start to become a bit chaotic, with too many people chipping in, a sharp reminder from a more senior resident ("It's still morning meeting") will immediately restore order. When the final song ends, signifying the end of the meeting, everyone cooperates in emptying the ashtrays near them, straightening the furniture which belongs in the living room and removing folding chairs which belong elsewhere. This all takes place within a few minutes and without any special orders being necessary. A few minutes later there is no evidence in the living room that a meeting with eighty to one hundred people has just taken place. Everyone is at his respective work.

WORK

Immediately after morning meeting everyone goes to his respective work areas—the kitchen crew to the kitchen, service crew and maintenance to their respective areas in the basement, community relations and communications departments to their offices. Each department begins the day with a brief department meeting of its own, generally run by the department head. Sometimes the coordinator of the department is in attendance too. If his department head is weak he will lend him support and after the meeting will give him advice on how to handle the department meeting better. Basically, though, it is the department head's responsibility.

The department meetings generally last only ten or fifteen minutes. Their main functions are to assign the work for the day, give out any instructions that may be necessary, issue warnings about unacceptable behavior or work practices which have been occurring, and perhaps most important, to encourage a feeling of solidarity within the department so that people can work moderately cheerfully together and feel that they can approach the more senior members of the department with their problems.

The nature of the work day varies from department to department. In the service crew it consists mainly of vacuuming and polishing floors, dusting furniture, cleaning windows, and the like. In the kitchen it consists of preparing food, serving meals, and cleaning up after them. In the communications department it involves office work, report writing, planning seminars, and arranging outside speaking engagements. In the business office responsibilities include typing letters to residents' probation officers and for other official house business, keeping residents' records filed and up to date, keeping office supplies for the whole house. In the expediting department it consists of manning the front desk, making fire runs, being available to the coordinator on duty and the house directors when people must be fetched and messages carried, and generally "policing" the house. In the community relations department it consists of finding possible donors for items needed by the house (through the department's own files of previous donations and also through the telephone book), making telephone calls to these businesses, and going out on the road to make personal calls and pickups.

The functions of the expediting department, headed by the chief expediter, have a special importance for the smooth running of the house. Expediters are the eyes and ears of the house, and also its conscience. They patrol the house looking for fires or breakages, for intruders or for residents who are doing anything they should not be doing; they act as messengers for the directors and coordinator on duty; they must know where every resident is in case they are told to fetch them; they find volunteers for clean-ups or pick people when necessary; they watch out for residents isolating themselves and tell them to "get involved"; they are supposed to be aware of residents who are "uptight" currently. To help in this they have a "Be Aware" book in the expediter's office in which an expediter who becomes aware of someone being uptight writes that resident's name. All expediters are supposed to read this book several times a day. Expediters could be loosely defined as the "police" of Daytop, but this term is not used because it has such negative connotations for Daytop residents. All residents are supposed to be aware of behavior that is not right and to make pull-ups to the person who makes a mistake, but expediters have a special obligation in this regard. Their work lasts the entire day and is especially stressful and tiring. Only by working in two shifts or by having scheduled off-duty periods for individuals (the system is changed periodically) is it at all workable.

Though the exact nature of the work varies greatly, certain features of work in Daytop can be stated quite generally. In the first place all the work in which residents are engaged is necessary for the welfare and survival of the House. Nobody is engaged in "occupational therapy," that is, work which has no purpose other than to occupy the worker and to train him in some way. Nor is anyone given "busy work," as commonly happens in prison and in the army. Even if someone is given extra work assignments for disciplinary or therapeutic reasons, he will be given work which has a genuine value, such as stripping and repolishing a bad floor, or laying stones to pave a dirt driveway. Work is always for the benefit of the group—not just for the benefit of the person doing it. Of course, it is for his benefit too. The fact that others depend on his work means that each resident can learn to associate work with social responsibility and that others care that he does it well.

With few exceptions, Daytop residents have had very poor work records and very irresponsible work habits. This is one of the prime areas in which they are supposed to be learning to change. For this reason a great emphasis is placed on high standards of performance in their work, on quality and consistency. In all departments and at all levels each resident has someone checking on his work performance and that person has someone checking on him, to insure that he (the supervisor) is enforcing the required standards upon his subordinates. There are, in theory, other organizations in which this kind of rigorous monitoring of work performance is supposed to take place, but it is doubtful whether there are many other examples of organizations where the monitoring is as frequent, thorough, and where the sanctions are so swift. For example, a meal being burned, delivered late, or otherwise unsatisfactory would usually lead to the department head of the kitchen being called into the coordinator's office for a stiff reprimand or "haircut." He in turn will reprimand the workers in his department, either calling them together specially or waiting until the next department meeting. The chain of reprimands may even be initiated by the house director calling the coordinator of the kitchen into his office for a reprimand.

Two justifications are given for this perfectionistic attitude to work in Daytop. One is that pride in work and in self are interrelated, and by demanding high standards of work in which a person can take pride, he can be helped to acquire more pride in himself. The other justification is that working under such pressures creates stress in the individual which he must learn to handle in the acceptable Daytop way, that is, in an adult and responsible way. Hitherto, most drug addicts have responded to stress situations only by running away.

When residents are assigned to their work departments, special care is taken not to assign individuals to work which is familiar and easy for them. Thus a former cook or restaurant worker would never be put in the kitchen, nor would a mechanic be put in the maintenance department—at least not initially.

The stress in work derives from many sources: the unfamiliarity of the work methods themselves (as we have just mentioned), the stern demands for quality and for work to be completed within a given time, the necessity of accepting orders without complaint, the necessity of working cooperatively with others, and the general requirement in Daytop to control one's impulses. In addition, a further source of stress derives from the fact that many residents are working under the supervision of more senior residents who are *themselves* operating at their own stress limits.

In Daytop residents must learn to deal with their feelings and to deal effectively with the stress which causes such feelings. Stress comes in many forms, but work-related stress has the advantage of being well structured and fairly obvious. When a person is not handling it effectively the source of such stress is fairly clear. Thus a person can be made aware relatively easily of what he is doing and why he is doing it. For example, if he made a hurtful remark to someone for no apparent reason this could be due to his being overwrought as a result of work-related stress. This does not justify the behavior, of course, but it helps to make it clear to the offender how he is getting into trouble by not dealing effectively with his stress.

Despite the strong emphasis on meeting work standards and production norms in Daytop, it is emphasized that work is a means to an end and not an end in itself. As it is often explained to a new resident, "If you don't do your work right you will hear about it. But if you are uptight talk to someone about it. Work is important, but it can wait." It might be thought that a guideline such as this would be open to much abuse by malingerers pretending to be uptight in order to get off work. In pratice though this rarely seems to happen. Far more common is the opposite complaint, that certain residents spend all their time engrossed in work and never make any effort to get involved with other people in Daytop, which is necessary if they are going to learn about themselves and change. The reason for this is that it is easier to work, even under these conditions, than to talk about problems that are causing one distress. It is very hard to get residents to talk about such things when they should. Very often they will only do so *after* they have got themselves into trouble by losing their temper or making some stupid mistake as a result of not dealing with the problem. Then they can be confronted heavily about the unacknowledged problem. Unfortunately residents sometimes prefer to split or run from the house at this point.

"Work" and "treatment" are closely integrated in Daytop. Work is one aspect of treatment. A resident is taught that high standards of work performance are demanded, but that when he is distressed, he can ask to be excused from work for a while in order to talk with an older resident. The stress from work is thought to be therapeutically valuable. Exploiting this idea even further, in Daytop full use is made of the fact that different jobs entail different kinds of stress, each having its own therapeutic possibilities. Therefore residents are moved from one job to another, as soon as they have mastered the stress presented by their earlier job. And in deciding which new jobs they should be given, the staff considers the personality needs of the individual and tries to give them a job in which the typical stresses and problems will demand qualities which he or she needs to develop and presently lacks.

No two people (including addicts) have the same personality problems but certain ones come up again and again: giving or taking orders, making pull-ups, discussing feelings, relating to the opposite sex, speaking in public, doing certain kinds of jobs. Daytop policy is to move people around to different jobs quite frequently so as to expose them to a great range of different stress situations. He or she stays in each position until it ceases to be a challenge. In this way all are forced to work through their problem areas instead of avoiding them.

To summarize, the work area is doubly important in terms of Daytop's rehabilitative goals: it is necessary vocational preparation in the form of both work habits and work skills; it is also a key part of the general therapeutic program, teaching better ways of dealing with stress, greater self-confidence, and the attitude that purposeful activity within normative limits can bring attainment of many of one's goals and, with that, real personal satisfaction.

SEMINAR

Every day after lunch, Monday through Friday, the whole house meets for seminar for one hour. Only coordinators and higher staff are exempt from this. Sometimes a resident will give a talk on a subject that interests him, or a visiting speaker will do this. At least once a week there is a mock speaking seminar in which residents practice giving talks about Daytop as if they were out on speaking engagements. This serves both as actual practice for those who will later go on speaking engagements and as a way of reinforcing everyone's understanding of the basic principles of Daytop. There are also other seminars which require impromptu speaking, such as debates, or "grab bag" seminars in which people are chosen to speak for five minutes on subjects drawn from a hat. Occasionally, a director will deliver a seminar on a philosophical topic related to the values of Daytop. This might be an analysis of the meaning of a passage from the Daytop Philosophy, a thought from the writings of Emerson, Bertrand Russell, or some other moral philosopher.

Another type of seminar is in the area of current affairs and political awareness. There was apparently an increase of emphasis in this area around 1968, partly through the regular seminars and partly through an independent series known as "intertwingle groups." These groups were smaller, involving only about ten residents at a time instead of the whole house. They were scheduled during work time and residents were released from work for the one hour per week. The intertwingle groups were begun by the teacher who was originally hired by Daytop for remedial education. As he was able to get additional teachers to help with that part of the educational work, he began the intertwingle groups to get residents thinking more about ideas. During the summer of 1968 this author took over the groups. Many of the topics were political in nature, and social criticism was certainly an important part of the curriculum.

One function of the seminar, as it is intended to operate, is to get residents to overcome their fears of speaking in front of others. This involves overcoming both their common fears about their inadequacy in using words and also their fears that what they will say will be laughed at or rejected. Seminars are also supposed to serve the function of encouraging residents to exercise their brains in thinking about abstract issues or ideas, entirely removed from the immediate daily realities of life in Daytop which necessarily occupy the greatest part of their waking thoughts.

In practice there is some conflict between these two major objectives (building self-confidence and exploring ideas) and one can see this in almost any seminar. Even when the seminar is planned as a talk, it is invariably run in a manner which permits a good deal of interchange with the audience—questions, comments, and contributions from all sides. Anyone giving a seminar who does not permit and achieve a considerable degree of audience involvement will be criticized on this score. "That wasn't a seminar. That was a lecture. Don't you know how a seminar is run?" This seems to be a point of ideological concern, as well as a pragmatic one that all those present need to feel involved in order to keep their attention and in order to get the practice in public speaking they need.

Some residents who have an especially noticeable problem with speaking up in front of others will have been told by their department head, coordinators, or other senior residents in groups or morning meeting that they must make a point of being heard in seminar. To the extent that they follow this advice—and they will be embarrassed into doing so if they are reluctant—it will happen that at least some of the people who raise their hands to speak in seminars do not have much to say in strictly intellectual terms. Perhaps the subject is over their heads, or they are still very inarticulate, or they are perhaps so burdened with the problems of survival in this difficult environment that they cannot focus their minds on the topic of the seminar. So, anyone delivering or participating in a seminar on a topic that really interested them could get very frustrated with these contributors. He must keep in mind that it is necessary for these people to work through their fears and difficulties in the area of public speaking and be tolerant of them. On the other hand if there are many of them at a given time, it may be necessary to be selective in calling upon participants who have their hands raised, in order to keep the theme of the seminar still in focus and to keep the interest of the others.

AFTER WORK

Work does not end at a fixed time, but when the day's assignment of work has been completed and the work area has been made clean and tidy. This applies equally to the kitchen, service crew and to the non-manual occupations such as community relations, business office, and communications. Kitchen, cooking stove, service crew closets, and office desks must all be left immaculate. They are checked at the end of the day by the department head and by the expediters, who report to the coordinator on duty. Most days they will also be checked by the coordinator of that department, for he or she is responsible and answerable for the performance of the department. When this "tightening up" is complete, residents may then congregate in the public areas of the house ("on the floor," as it is termed) to socialize. They may drink coffee, play records or (if the weather is fine) stroll outside while talking to others.

"Isolating" oneself is taboo in Daytop. Rarely will anyone be seen reading a book by himself, though occasionally an older resident will be seen reading a newspaper or magazine. There is a television room where the set is playing for several hours most evenings, but new residents had better not be found in here and even older ones had better not appear to spend too much time here. After work residents are supposed to be "getting involved" with their peers, especially by talking to those with more Daytop experience in order to learn from them and conversely by talking to those newer than themselves in order to "pull them in." One of the functions of the expediters is to find any residents who are isolating themselves and either send someone to talk to them (if they are very new) or send them to find someone to talk to. "Get involved" is the cry of the expediter.

Three evenings a week (Monday, Wednesday and Friday) encounter groups are held, so there is not a great deal of loose time after work is finished. On Tuesday and Thursday, however, there is the whole evening for socializing. On Sunday most of the day is "loose." Often, though, there will be an organized volleyball game or some similar activity. There will be overwhelming pressure for everyone—or at least all the men—to join in. Only those with considerable seniority can escape this pressure. Again, it is the job of the expediters to round up all residents when something like this is organized.

By and large, after-work time is not defined as being available for relaxing but more as being for "relating," that is, getting to know fellow residents on a person-to-person basis. It is held to be especially important for residents who work together to relate in this way. There are generally some hostile feelings between people who work together under pressure and they tend to see each other only in terms of their work relationship. Yet because of the strain they are under while working, they need the understanding of their work associates. This is true both for those who are on the same status level within the department and also for those in a superior–subordinate relationship. Department heads, department coordinators, and other relatively senior members of any department are expected to extend themselves to get to know the more junior people in their department and to help them to deal with the problems they are experiencing. Equally, the newer residents are supposed to ask to speak to their older colleagues when they feel in need of help or simply when they feel uptight without necessarily knowing the reason.

No one is allowed to go to bed early without permission. Before the general bedtime there is a final "tighten up." Members of the service crew plus other residents designated by the expediters clean all ashtrays, empty and reline all garbage cans throughout the three floors of the house and basement, and tidy up anything which has been displaced during the course of the evening.

It would be wrong to leave the impression that Daytop residents are *never* allowed to relax—that work and relating occupies every waking moment. However, it is the working assumption of Daytop staff, sometimes made explicit, that ex-junkies do not know how to use leisure time in a positive way. Hence they are given only a limited amount of it and they are under supervision even then. Daytop is struggling to extinguish the habits of the junkie, including his tendency to retreat into a capsule of "negative" reminiscences and self-indulgent fantasies.

SATURDAY "OPEN HOUSE"

After morning meeting on Saturday everyone goes to work to "G.I." the whole house—sleeping rooms, offices, public areas, kitchen, basement—the entire house.

(This term derives from the Army, where a General Inspection [G.I.] is the occasion for the most meticulous cleaning, polishing, and tidying of one's quarters. From its original status as a noun, "G.I." has come to be used exclusively as a verb in Daytop.)

Open House is held most Saturday evenings. Members of the general public who have telephoned the house in advance to make reservations arrive about eight o'clock in the evening. The house is immaculate and the residents themselves, showered, tidied, and in their best clothes, are also looking their best. This weekly event brings out a mixture of feelings. These include feelings of relief that the hard work of the week, culminating in the Saturday "GI-ing" of the house, is over and there are feelings of nervousness about meeting members of the "straight" or "square" world. But there are also feelings of pride and pleasure for those who have learned to overcome their fears to some extent and to enjoy entertaining visitors in "their" house, as respectable and self-respecting persons—living a very different way of life from the one they knew on "the streets."

After all the visitors for that particular Saturday evening Open House have arrived and been greeted at the front desk, signed the visitors' book, and been shown into the house, the first part of Open House begins with a sit-down event. This is usually presided over by a director or assistant director. The format of this occasion varies, though it usually begins with the reading of the Philosophy and will include a short celebration of "Concept birthdays." If a resident of the House or staff member has completed one or more years "in the Concept" during the past week (and provided that they are considered deserving on the basis of their recent conduct) they will be called forward to be congratulated, to hear a brief "this is your life" summary of their career in the House, and to make a short speech. This speech usually revolves around the theme of what difficult times they have had in surviving in Daytop and living up to the standards demanded, how many times they almost gave up hope and how much they owe to the concern shown to them by fellow residents. Brief though it is, this birthday ceremony is usually a rather poignant one.

Open House serves several functions for Daytop. It introduces members of the public to Daytop and what it is doing, thus contributing to good public relations. From the residents' point of view, Open House brings them into contact with members of the "square" world and helps to prepare them for reentry back into outside society as responsible citizens. Most residents in Daytop report that they "go through changes" (that is, they experience a lot of fears and anxieties) in connection with Open House. They have fears about how the visitors will look at them, fearing that they will look down on them. Invariably, however because they have learned to be frank and open about their past and to act as if they positively accept the values and philosophy of Daytop as they explain it to the visitors, they make overwhelmingly favorable impressions. New residents of less than a month in the House must be escorted by an older peer throughout the evening. This chaperoning arrangement is designed to teach them the expected behavior for Open House, and so protect them from the extreme fears of coping with a totally strange situation. It also serves to protect the visitors from contact with totally unsocialized addicts who might embarrass them and give them a bad impression of Daytop as well.

Many residents soon learn to play the role of host at Open House with considerable competence and come to enjoy the good feelings from it. In some cases the experience becomes a total "ego trip" in which the Daytop resident elicits the admiration of his audience of one or several visitors for the enormity of the change he has made in his outlook on life, for pulling himself up by his own bootstraps. This, told against the background of graphic descriptions of former delinquencies, can make an unforgettable impact on the naive visitor.

Up to a point, the gratification a resident receives for this is considered beneficial, insofar as it reinforces his still shaky commitment to Daytop values and gives him good feelings about himself, linked to his new values. It is recognized, however, that this can easily get out of hand—especially when the listener is an attractive member of the opposite sex. It is the special responsibility of the expediters to patrol the floor relentlessly and be aware of how all residents are behaving. If they suspect that a particular resident is spending too long talking to attractive young guests of the opposite sex, they will intervene and suggest to the resident that he is needed elsewhere. Should he be foolish enough not to take the hint at once, it will be repeated more insistently and he can expect stern disciplinary action after Open House is over. House directors place so much importance on good behavior at Open House that—even though no visitors may be aware of any untoward behavior—invariably after every Open House there are reprimands for individuals and usually for the expediting staff collectively.

On the whole, however, residents get many good feelings from Open House. After the guests have gone home, the residents often continue to party by themselves until late into the night. Then everyone pitches in to clean up the dining room, living room, and kitchen and a feeling of strong group solidarity is generated before everyone goes to bed, well and truly tired. Next day, Sunday, is the one day of the week when residents may stay in bed late. Sunday is a "loose" day, aside from the need to prepare and clean up from two meals. There is enough time, though, for relaxation, playing cards, volleyball, listening to music, and so forth. This revitalizes everyone just enough to face the beginning of another week full of the demands that are so big a part of the Daytop way of life.

FORMAL STRUCTURE

We have outlined the main features of the typical day and the typical week in Daytop. In order to complete our account of the framework of organization of the Daytop community, we must explain the formal division of labor between departments and the hierarchy of status and authority.

The larger departments are: kitchen, service crew, operations (maintenance and landscaping), community relations, expediting, and SPAN (the outreach project to help addicts living in and around Manhattan's Lower East Side to work their way into Daytop). Each of these departments has between seven and fourteen workers assigned to it. Smaller departments are generally grouped with a larger department under the supervision of one coordinator. These arrangements change from time to time. The housekeeping department (mending, and ironing clothes, making drapes, etc.) is usually headed by women. The commissary is usually linked with the kitchen. Other small departments are communications, business office, medical, warehouse, and automotive. Each of the larger departments has a department head and under him is a "ramrod."

The "ramrod," as his title might suggest, is expected to push the department's workers to make sure that work assignments are completed on time. As one department head said to a resident who was asking for the ramrod's position and thought he was doing the job already, "You've got to blow that good guy act. A ramrod is a *bad* guy." In general, then, the ramrod is the first-line supervisor who pushes the rank-and-file workers into meeting production norms, while the department head is responsible for planning the work and talking to department workers about their personal problems, especially those related to the work situation. The coordinator oversees the department head, helps and teaches him to do his job properly, and steps in to handle areas where he is still incompetent. There is much variation in this balance of power and functions between coordinator, department head, and ramrod according to the personality, competence, and other commitments of each. On days when the coordinator takes his turn at overseeing the whole house as "coordinator on duty," he has to depend heavily on his head of department to keep things running well for he is still responsible for that department.

Each department has a coordinator over the department head, SPAN excepted. SPAN and certain other departments are considered to have higher status than other departments. This correlates with the longer time residents usually have to spend in Daytop before being assigned to these higher status departments. Aside from SPAN, the higher status departments are community relations and expediting. A resident who was given a job change from department head of kitchen to ordinary worker in community relations would thus be considered as taking a step forward in his Daytop career. Similarly, a job change from service crew to operations would be a step up, as would a transfer from kitchen or service crew to expediting. The status relationships between departments are shown approximately in Figure One.

Among coordinators relative status is not necessarily related in any simple or obvious way to the status of their departments. It is more related to their seniority. Out of some nine or so coordinators, one is designated senior coordinator. Instead of supervising a department his main responsibility is to train the newer coordinators. The newest of them are designated coordinator-trainees, but the senior coordinator is responsible for helping *all* coordinators to learn their roles. In addition to the supervision of their departments, coordinators take turns at being "coordinator on duty" for a day at a time. The COD may be compared to the officer of the watch on a ship; he is completely responsible to the house director for the smooth running of the house. He arranges prospect interviews, considers requests for permission of various kinds, conducts the morning meeting of the whole house, handles outside phone calls, decides upon disciplinary measures (except in the most serious cases) and administers them, and so forth.

The coordinator's office is the command center of the house. This is the place where prospect interviews are held. Expediters hurry to and from the coordinator's office relaying messages and orders. Apart from the COD at most times there

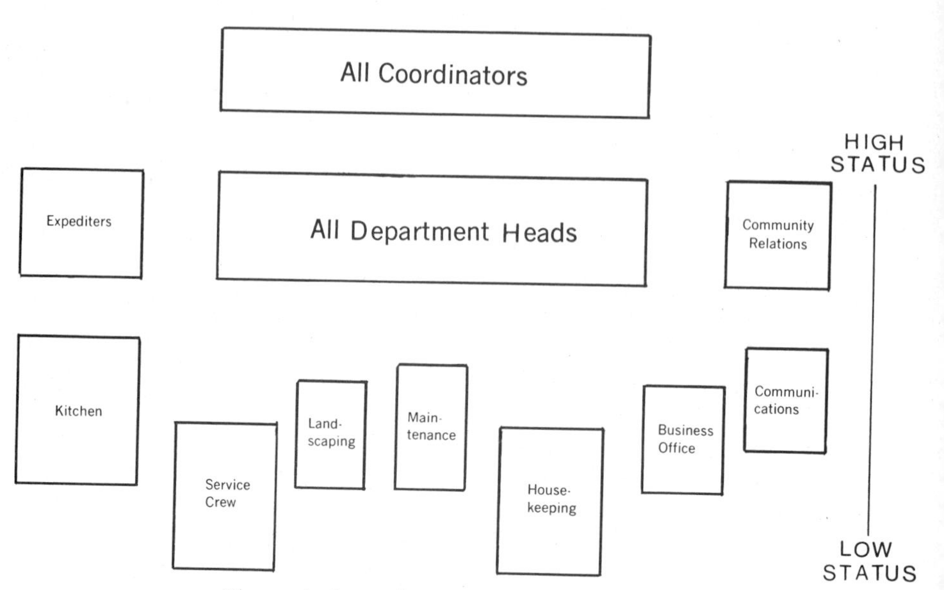

Figure 1. Status hierarchy among departments.

are one or more other coordinators present. This mitigates the proverbial "loneliness of leadership" as they offer suggestions and criticisms to help the COD. The next day their roles will be reversed. Among the coordinators especially, but also at many other levels within Daytop, a person performs his roles under the scrutiny of peers who are supposed to offer helpful suggestions and constructive criticism, while he is encouraged to ask for help. This is not a sharing of *responsibility* for the individual remains personally responsible for his performance and his decisions. It is, however, an effective way of learning new roles and responsibilities, both on account of the utility of the actual advice and on account of the pressure not to slide out of doing difficult and unfamiliar things which are being faced for the first time.

There are some other positions of importance which should be described. The "guru" ranks equal to a coordinator but instead of having departmental responsibilities of the coordinator, his job is to be a full-time counselor to residents and to be an expert in the philosophy of Daytop. He has his own room in the basement of the house. There he can meet with individual residents at their request or with groups that he convenes specially. Routinely, he has the task of setting up encounter groups and deciding which residents shall be put together in the same groups. He also convenes "specials" or encounter groups among some subgroup (usually a department) in which relationships have deteriorated. The "coordinator of women" assisted by the "head of women," fulfills a very similar role for the females in the house, known collectively as "the women's dynamic."

In charge of the whole house is a director and assistant director or, occasionally,

The staff confers in the Coordinators' Office, the main command post of the house.

two co-directors. In charge of the entire Daytop operation of two (later to be four) houses is the executive director, assisted by a number of corporation directors, and subject to the broad oversight of the Board of Directors of Daytop Village, Incorporated, including the Medical-Psychiatric Superintendant. We show this hierarchy in Figure Two.

The Executive Director (David Deitch) has under him the directors of the individual houses, and an Associate Executive Director whose main function is to serve as liaison with funding sources and other agencies upon whose goodwill Daytop depends. He also has several corporation directors. These are senior staff members, including one of the two staff members who came with him originally (the other left) and the first leaders to emerge from among Daytop residents. The latter became the first house directors after Deitch himself stepped down from that position to be full-time executive director. When they, in turn, were replaced as house directors by a new wave of rising leaders, they were promoted to the newly-created status of corporation directors. Their duties are not

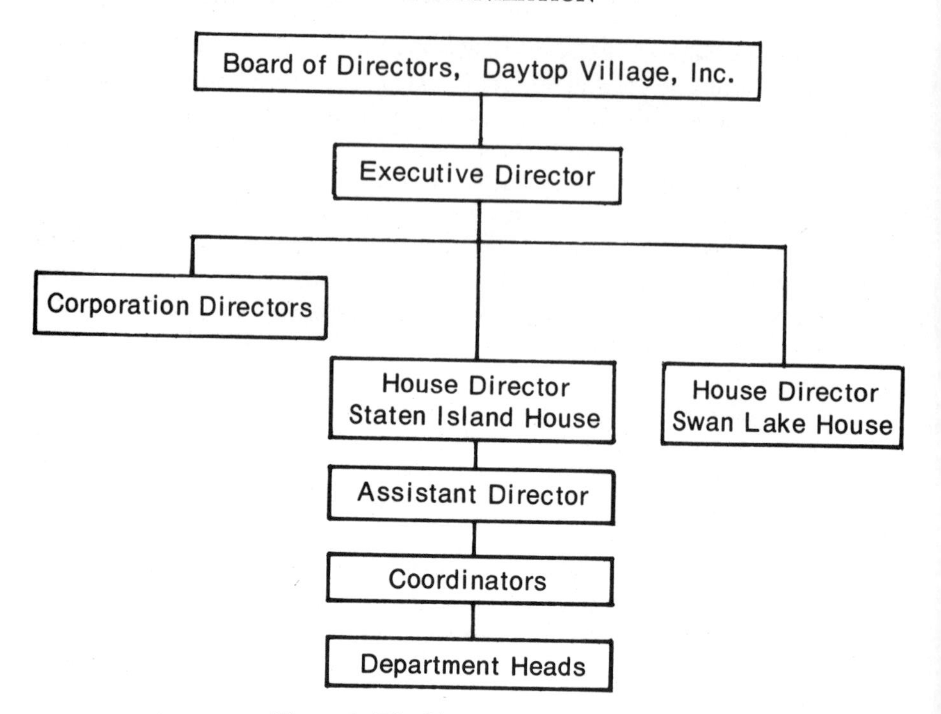

Figure 2. The hierarchy of authority.

fixed but change from time to time as Deitch decides. Some tasks which are known to have been handled by corporation directors are: making preparations for opening a new house, public relations projects, keeping an eye on one of the existing houses in absence of the Executive Director, establishing and running the "intensive training institutes" for other professionals and agencies, and so forth.

By virtue of their seniority, their roles in the establishment of Daytop, and close association with David Deitch, corporation directors are held in some awe by residents. Collectively the corporation directors are known as the "core group." Periodically this group meets to discuss issues of policy—therapeutic, administrative, and political. It may be surmised that most of the input of new ideas comes from Deitch himself. Some informants close to this group gave me their impressions that in those discussions Deitch's views would invariably prevail, due to the intense feelings of loyalty and need for his approval felt by all the others. That these feelings should exist is hardly surprising in view of the fact that they each owe their personal salvation to his concern, dedication, and talent.

Most weekdays, in the late morning, the house director or his assitant director hold a meeting of all coordinators. This is known as the "A.M." meeting even when it happens to take place in the afternoon. There is no predetermined agenda. If the house director has something to say to his staff, he will do so. After this each coordinator in turn has a chance to bring up for discussion any matters that he wishes. The director sits in a highbacked swivel chair. In front of him is a large round coffee table, similar to the one in the coordinator's office. The others attending the meeting sit around the room in armchairs, on sofas, or on folding chairs.

Each coordinator has a notebook or clipboard with notes on his lap, and generally has come prepared with a list of matters for discussion. Usually each takes notes on the proceedings as they develop. This is expected behavior, and someone who does not take notes or who came without paper and pen would probably be challenged about it. There is no official recording secretary and no minutes are circulated.

The kind of business which is discussed seems to fall mainly into the following areas: matters affecting the house as a whole, for example organizing a system for handling cash donations offered by visitors at the Saturday night Open House; matters requiring special cooperation between departments; concerns the director might have, where he may lay down some demands for better performance by all staff, especially when the house is drifting into a period of relative "looseness" or laxness; clinical discussions of individual residents who are being exceptionally troublesome or who are presenting problems in some way out of the ordinary; requests put forward by members of the different departments through their coordinator for various privileges, for example a phone call, a letter home, recovery of some personal possessions.

If the director chooses to decide unilaterally about any of these matters, that is the end of the discussion. He has the authority to do so, and it is unlikely that his coordinators would present any problem of compliance even if he often chose to make decisions that way. Most times, however, he will invite staff to express themselves and to defend their ideas against challenge from him or their peers. This serves the educational function of giving them experience in decision-making, helping them to make better decisions within their own spheres as coordinators—as well as in their personal lives. After coordinators have made their suggestions and discussed each other's ideas, either the director will make the decision in the light of this input, or he may ask for a vote. If the problem lies within the purview of a certain coordinator, and he has brought it up to get help with the decision, it may be tossed back to him by the director to make the decision himself. In the latter case the discussion may have helped him to clarify his thoughts, or the function of this meeting may simply be to force him to face up to making the decision himself. Sometimes there is real uncertainty as to whether a coordinator has the authority to make a certain kind of decision on his own. So there is the dual problem of helping them to learn how far their authority extends and how to exercise it with assurance and good sense. The house director's A.M. meeting serves these teaching functions as well as the administrative and clinical functions of getting certain decisions made and keeping the operation of the house under continuous review.

Most of the personnel who keep Daytop functioning are themselves in training and in treatment. They are learning and performing their exacting roles under the supervision of only three supervisors. These three are the house director, assistant director, and senior coordinator, all Daytop "confirmees" (or graduates) and salaried staff. These three, aided sporadically by the Executive Director or one of the corporation directors, regulate this community of eighty to one hundred former drug addicts, many of whom are not far removed from the streets (forty percent had been in Daytop under six months).

Yet these three are not seen by the average resident as much as the coordinators are. Only occasionally does one of the salaried staff look in on morning meeting or participate in a disciplinary action for an individual. They do appear on some occasions of major importance such as a special house meeting.

The awe of the average resident towards the house director and his immediate colleagues derives, one infers, in part from the perceived respect and awe in which the coordinators (who are themselves looked up to by the residents) hold these very senior Daytop personnel. Also, residents become aware of the power which directors have, not only over them, but over the coordinators who seem, at other times, to be so powerful themselves. A director, after all, can assign a coordinator to a new department or strip him of his status. Although the most senior personnel in the hierarchy of the particular house are not much seen by the average resident, they soon become aware of their importance. Coordinators, of course, are constantly aware of the existence of this top level of staff for they answer to them daily.

This relationship of supervision and teaching is Daytop's last stage of treatment for her residents. Coordinators will have already spent one period of time working in the SPAN office and getting used to being in the outside world again. After their spell of duty as coordinators they will then spend another period back in SPAN or working outside and spending nine-tenths of their time away from the house. Then they should be ready for confirmation. In SPAN they are also under the supervision of the SPAN Director, so that the "finishing school" is continuous, whether in the house or outside. At least until one is confirmed, the Daytop experience is one of teaching and learning, giving orders and taking them, helping others and being helped by others.

4/Social controls

In the preceding chapters we have described the culture of Daytop or, as it is known locally, "the Concept," and we have shown that a very high level of conformity to its normative standards is generally maintained. In this chapter we now turn to look at the means through which this high level of conformity is achieved and maintained.

As in all successful systems, there are in Daytop various arrangements for detecting and calling attention to deviant behavior as well as arrangements which tend to preclude its taking place. Among the arrangements which tend to prevent deviance are: teaching the norms and rules to new members, attaching rewards to behavior which conforms to them and negative sanctions to behavior that is deviant. In Daytop, though, these arrangements are particularly highly developed —for the same reasons that the norms and rules themselves are very explicit (basically that the behavior expected in Daytop is far removed from that typical of Daytop residents when they were "on the street").

The monitoring of residents' behavior in Daytop is facilitated by a number of ecological factors in the living arrangements. The movements of residents are very strictly regulated: they are not allowed out of the house onto the grounds without checking out; they are not allowed off the grounds except on authorized business in the company of senior residents; and within the house nearly all their time is spent either in working or socializing in public view. On the premise that most deviant behavior takes place in secret, the living arrangements of Daytop are deliberately arranged to keep privacy to a minimum.

Observation of deviant behavior is, however, only the first step in its regulation. It is necessary that someone call the attention of the deviant to the fact that his behavior violates specified norms of the group. Someone should then report the occurrence of this deviant behavior to persons in authority who can determine whether any further steps are called for. We have mentioned already how the "responsible concern" norm requires each resident to confront and pull-up his peers when he suspects them of deviant conduct. The existence of such a norm, by itself, does not of course guarantee that this will be done. However, so long as there are within the house a minimum number of residents who act according to these norms, residents who fail to confront, pull-up their peers, and report misconduct know that they take the risk of being reported themselves for misconduct. Even without assuming any degree of internalized commitment to the values of

Daytop, someone who wants to make his stay in Daytop as tolerable as possible and who is aware of the vast range of positive and negative sanctions at the disposal of those who run Daytop, is likely to calculate just on the basis of expediency that he should conform a good part of the time. It is also highly relevant here that many drug addicts have a strong need to feel socially accepted. They soon realize that acceptance in Daytop is contingent upon conformity to the norms of the Daytop Concept, which includes as a major feature making pull-ups and reporting other residents who will not accept pull-ups or conform to basic norms. Just a few people conforming even part of the time by exposing the misconduct of their peers allows considerable surveillance of the average Daytop resident.

In addition to this general surveillance of each other's conduct, special responsibilities for monitoring the conduct of all residents is assigned to certain people. The expediting department has such a responsibility and so have all residents who hold any kind of status in the house—whether it is based on an official title such as department head or coordinator, or whether it is based on length of time in the house and the possession of certain privileges on the strength of this. Residents in the latter categories are known as "strength" and, in return for the status accorded them and the privileges they enjoy over other residents (which we shall discuss shortly), they are expected to set a good example.

SANCTIONS

We now turn to examine some of the many positive and negative sanctions in common use in Daytop. To look first at positive sanctions or rewards, we find that these most often take the form of granting someone's request for a "privilege." On entering Daytop a resident is required to give up many of the rights which are taken for granted by people outside. He or she gives up all personal possessions, including money or other valuables such as jewelry and watches. These are put into safe keeping for the owner. While he stays at Daytop, he also loses the right to come and go at will, the right to have visitors or to receive communications by phone or mail from outside the house. These rights which are surrendered become the basis for "privileges" to be granted for good conduct in Daytop.

Another significant reward in Daytop is promotion to jobs carrying more responsibility and higher status: from ordinary worker to "ramrod" of the department, to expediter, to department head, to coordinator-trainee, finally perhaps even to house director. These "labels" and the positions they designate in the Daytop social system carry graduated degrees of status and respect, proportional to the amount of responsibility and power which go with them. Just as promotion up this ladder is one of the major forms of positive sanction for good conduct and demonstrated commitment to Daytop values, so demotion (which is not at all infrequent) is one of the most severe negative sanctions. Being "shot down" or demoted may result either from making serious errors in the management of one's work responsibilities or for flagrant misconduct in one's personal affairs; for instance, lying or stealing, making a phone call without permission, and so forth. It is rare (but not by any means unknown) for a coordinator or anyone above that level to be "shot down," but up to and including the level of department head it is quite common.

Position in the status hierarchy serves as a reward or a package of rewards in two respects: first, there is a correlation between status or rank and the degree of privileges a resident is allowed (including the amount of contact he is allowed with people outside of Daytop, the amount of menial work he is required to do, and the amount of "walk-around money" that he receives); second, the position he is awarded signifies the evaluation that the house director and those who advise him have made of the individual's performance in the house—it indicates how well they feel he is progressing and serves as a cue to other residents, affecting the way they see him and hence his prestige in the house.

Daytop has an elaborate status system, that is, a system of rewards that serve both as symbols of prestige within the group and as concrete privileges that make life more comfortable for those who are permitted to have them. The new resident just in the door a few days ago is at the bottom of the status system. This is reflected in the menial nature of his first work assignments—dishwashing if he is in the kitchen, toilet cleaning if he is in the service crew. It is also reflected in the fact that his name appears at the bottom of the "pop sheet" which lists the residents in order of date of entry. Residents in their first month are designated on the list as "noodleheads," though this name is heard very little. Male residents do not normally get a bed and a room right away but sleep on a couch in the living room for at least a few days and possibly for a couple of weeks. This is partly for the practical reason that beds are often not available, but also for the symbolic purpose of making the point that one *earns* everything in Daytop—even one's bed. While there are new residents sleeping in the living room an older brother known as the "night owl" stays up to keep an eye on them and talk to them, if necessary.

As a resident gains experience and his name moves up the pop sheet, he learns that he may ask for certain privileges. Some are conventionally given before others would be considered. Letters home are allowed before a visit home, an escorted visit (accompanied by an older resident) before a solo visit, and a day visit before a whole weekend. Other privileges which can often be earned in the first six months include the following: possession of some items of personal clothing brought in the house when a resident entered or possession of other personal items (not including watches or jewelry yet), permission to grow sideburns for males, permission to go out on house movie trips or other pleasure excursions for limited groups, and permission to read, watch occasional television, or play a musical instrument. When I first moved into the house as a resident, other residents guessed immediately that I was not a genuine resident from the fact that I had been allowed to keep my watch, wedding band, and sideburns. An ordinary resident first entering Daytop would automatically have these taken away from him.

At the top of the status hierarchy, a house director or corporation director has freedom of work hours, deciding for himself when he will work and what tasks he will delegate to others. He can also have all kinds of personal service should he desire it. Merely by calling the expediting office he can have food prepared especially for him and brought up to his office, he can have his bed made, his clothes sent out for dry cleaning and picked up for him, his car washed—almost anything he can think of that requires only semiskilled labor can be done for him as well as some things requiring more skill if it happens to be available in the house.

Within departments there is a status system reflected in job assignments, aside from the obvious status positions of department head and ramrod. In the kitchen, for example, when a worker is ready to be promoted from the dishpan, he will not be allowed to cook lunch right away but will start with breakfast. After serving as breakfast cook he may be promoted to lunch cook, then after serving in that capacity for a while he may be assigned to cooking dinner.

Most residents fear to leave Daytop, either because jail terms await them should they split or because they fear that they cannot physically survive much longer if they return to their former way of life. Remaining in Daytop is hard, though, both because of the strict discipline and because of the lack of certain freedoms which residents formerly took for granted. There are two ways in which residents can make their stay in Daytop more tolerable. They can decide to conform outwardly with enthusiasm and earn themselves some privileges which will make life more comfortable. Then, later, they can decide to go further and accept the norms and values as standards which they really attempt to apply to themselves, so that their deprivations and struggles have some positive meaning for them. It is worth noting that even the more cautious adjustment to Daytop (the former one) entails cooperating with the social control system.

When we consider negative sanctions in Daytop, we find an amazing variety of methods for indicating disapproval of something a resident has done. It is important to note that negative sanctions are never presented as punishments in Daytop but rather as "learning experiences," designed to teach the recipient that a certain form of behavior is unacceptable in Daytop and bad for him. When a learning experience is given out, it is always accompanied by a clear explanation of the reason why—in terms of the kinds of personal changes the resident is supposed to be making—he must learn to avoid this kind of behavior. Usually when a learning experience is given, the recipient is called before a couple of coordinators and other residents including his peers and told forcefully what he has been doing wrong. The kind of learning experience he receives is carefully tailored not just to the specific offense, but to the nature of the personality problem underlying it and is designed to help him overcome it. This point should become clearer as we catalog some of the major forms of learning experience and give some examples of negative sanctions. The commonest by far is the individual pull-up from a fellow resident, which we have mentioned in an earlier chapter.

The *pull-up* can be illustrated by the following small incident which was observed. A, B, and C, plus the writer were sitting in a group talking. A got up to leave, and in doing so, she dropped some cigarette ash on the floor. B and C, both new residents, almost simultaneously called her attention to it. As they did so, both looked noticeably pleased with themselves. A thanked them and picked up the ash carefully, smiling with pleasure herself. It is possible that all three residents were affected by the presence of the observer-writer and were, in a sense, putting on a show. But—even if this is true—it is unimportant, first because we shall use this example to illustrate the pattern of *expected* behavior, and second because most of the time in Daytop residents are in fact under the observation of others. This is the typical social situation in which Daytop residents find themselves.

This simple example illustrates several features of the pull-up. First, the rule is that one does not correct the mistake for the other person but calls his attention to it so that he can correct it himself. Second, the pull-up is made out loud, not in a confidential whisper—and if others are present to witness it, so much the better. The embarrassment of the recipient is felt to be a useful aid in remembering not to repeat that mistake. Third, pull-ups are designed for the benefit of the person receiving them, to help him remember the rules he has been forgetting and to encourage him to conform to them. There are, of course, benefits to the person who makes the pull-up: it tends to make him look good in the eyes of senior residents, it tends to strengthen his identification with the normative order of Daytop and it also "toughens his belly" as he forces himself to do something which most residents find hard, since they fear that when they give someone a pull-up that person will dislike them. Hard as it is for new residents to accept, the pull-up is indeed for the benefit of the person receiving it and both are expected to keep this in mind. The person who gives the pull-up is supposed to give it in a way that is forceful enough but not vindictive; the person receiving it is expected to take it with good grace and to acknowledge that it is for his benefit by saying "thank you." When a resident feels that someone who gave him a pull-up was really getting his own back for some earlier grievance, taking out his general frustrations, or in some other way "coming out sick," he can take the matter to an encounter group and thrash it out verbally with the other person. At the time of the pull-up, though, he must accept it graciously and thank the person who gave it to him.

Because of their frequency, pull-ups are the main form of negative sanction or negative reinforcement in Daytop. They provide a relatively easy, effective, and rapid way for residents to learn normative expectations. Without pull-ups, in fact, learning to modify self-destructive behavior patterns would be a much longer and more arduous task. The learning of new behavior presents great difficulty, of course, for it entails breaking personal habits which may be of long standing and modifying personality traits which may be strongly ingrained. Residents who are careless, untidy, or insensitive to other people will find themselves receiving the most pull-ups, and they will find that the degree of embarrassment will escalate until their conduct improves. Provoking embarrassment is used very deliberately as a learning aid in Daytop. For example, one day, halfway through lunch, Mel came into the dining room. Loudly he said, "Can I have your attention please. I was very stupid. I forgot to check in again. I'm sorry." Everyone paused to listen to him. Obviously it was painful for him to make this announcement, one that he had been instructed to make. "OK Mel," someone said and the general conversation resumed.

Pull-ups exist in Daytop to teach something to the people who receive them. They are considered to be for their personal benefit in the long run—though they may not appreciate it at the time. They are also for the benefit of the group as a whole, for life in Daytop would be much different and on the whole less agreeable if people freely went around leaving dirty plates behind them, forgetting to complete jobs they had begun, leaving lights on, forgetting to return tools to their proper place, neglecting to deliver messages left with them, and so forth. When pull-ups are brought into morning meeting this is one of the common themes of elaborations (that everyone has a vested interest in helping each individual to act more responsibly), though it seems that only residents who have been around a considerable time and achieved some position of responsibility are capable of grasping this point and keeping it in mind. On a less sophisticated level, more residents are able to appreciate the fact that a pull-up taken care of at the time, when they can see the mistake, is far less trouble to them than it is to let it go uncorrected and then have to endure the inconvenience of searching out the culprit and having him rectify the mistake later. This is another theme of morning meeting elaborations—that people could save themselves a lot of trouble if they were more conscientious in watching their fellows and making pull-ups when necessary. As an example, if one person who sleeps in a certain room forgets to make his bed, it is likely that all the other occupants of the room will be required to clean and tidy the room over again. This clearly gives each of them an incentive to check up on all of his fellows.

The pull-up epitomizes all of the main features of a learning experience in Daytop, though others which we shall discuss shortly may be more dramatic. All learning experiences are designed to help someone change his self-destructive behavior; all learning experiences are administered by a person's peers, which is not only more effective for him but is also beneficial for them; both giving and receiving learning experiences is the common experience of life in Daytop; and failing to play one's role properly in administering a learning experience to a fellow is treated like any other failure to behave in the required way—one may receive a pull-up for failing to make an earlier pull-up properly or for failing to make one at all.

An example of how forceful a pull-up can be is provided by the following observation. One night, around one A.M., after most of the house has been in bed for about half an hour, we are awakened by a voice shouting, "Everyone into the bathroom." All of the male residents of the largest wing of the building, bleary-eyed, are crowded into the bathroom they use. The night expediter is holding an ashtray holding one cigarette butt and asking, "Whose is this?" It was found in this bathroom after bedtime. In a broken voice, Louie says faintly, "It's mine."

"Let's all thank Louie for getting us up," says the expediter and an obliging chorus of ironical voices chants, "Thank you, Louie."

As if this is a familiar ritual, the expediter continues, "Good night, all." And a chorus responds, "Good night, Louie."

For repeated offenses or more serious ones, a verbal reprimand or *haircut* will be administered. A typical offense for which a haircut would be given is "reacting," that is, refusing to accept a pull-up or direction in the expected manner—politely and without complaint. In a case such as this, the resident whose pull-up or direction was reacted to is expected to initiate a complaint to the chief expediter or the "shingle" expediter on duty. He will attempt to verify the report by calling in any reliable witnesses for brief questioning and, when he is satisfied that the offense really did take place a haircut is "booked." How much confirmation is required from other sources will depend on several factors, including the standing in the house of the complainant and the reputation of the alleged offender—if he is known to have been perpetrating a series of such offenses recently, extensive confirmation will not be required. When a haircut is booked, details are passed on to the coordinator on duty who scrutinizes them to satisfy himself that the offense truly merits a haircut. Sometimes the COD disallows a haircut that is booked, as being unsubstantiated or not sufficiently serious or because he has other plans for dealing with the offender.

When a haircut is to be given, the COD selects a cross-section of residents to help him administer it, including some other senior residents, the aggrieved party and one or more residents who are close friends of the offender. These names will be telephoned down to the expediter's office and a message will be broadcast over the public address system for these people to report to the coordinator's office. When they arrive they will be briefed by the COD as to who is to receive the haircut and for what general pattern of bad behavior, including the specific incident complained of. The expediters then summon the person who is to receive the haircut. When he reports to the coordinator's office, he finds the door is closed, which signifies to him with a fair degree of certainty the reason why he is being called there.

When a person walks into his haircut, he is faced by a semicircle of seated figures and told to stand up against the door. Then, in a prearranged sequence, each person in the semicircle delivers a tirade of verbal abuse at high volume, castigating the behavior which led to his appearance here. He will be called a "stupid asshole" and similar names. It will be pointed out to him that he is acting like a baby, which is what he came here to change. He will be warned that if he doesn't change this behavior forthwith sterner consequences will follow. He will be reminded that this kind of behavior is what got him into trouble in the first place and led to his being here. Through all of this the person receiving the haircut must remain silent and deferential. Generally the last person to speak is the coordinator-on-duty himself. When he has finished he dismisses the recipient of the haircut without his being permitted to say a word. The recipient knows, however, that he may deal with the hostile feelings which this experience invariably produces by taking the persons he feels most angry towards to the next encounter group where he can scream back at them to his heart's content. Meanwhile, he must grit his teeth and take his medicine. After the haircut is over, he will not be shunned by his fellows. It is made very clear that it is the stupid behavior which is being rejected and not the person. He is expected to talk about his haircut and to explain what he did to deserve it. He is expected to talk about it in a "positive" way, not justifying himself but showing that he is trying to learn from his mistake.

The effects of a haircut on the deviant individual himself seem to be strong. In spite of the fact that some residents "switch off" when receiving a haircut, even for them it can scarcely avoid being a beneficial experience. We should not forget, though, the effects of the haircut on those who help to administer it. It is a hard thing for them to do, especially for those who are close friends of the deviant. It is important that they do take part in the haircut for two major reasons. First, this places them on one side of the fence, identifying them by their words and behavior with the normative order of Daytop. It makes it virtually impossible for them to commiserate with the deviant afterwards or to help him justify his behavior in any way. If anyone who is selected to participate in giving out the haircut fails to perform his role in a satisfactory way, he will himself receive a haircut from the coordinator on duty and other senior members of the group after the door has closed behind the original offender.

Within this structure it is very hard for residents to maintain the kind of "inmate solidarity" against the institutional regime which is typical of jails and most rehabilitative or educational institutions. On a psychological level, participation in the haircut helps the resident who is beginning to modify his behavior patterns to internalize the new values more thoroughly as he vocally rejects those aspects of his former self which he sees reflected in the deviant standing in front of the door. Other participants in the haircut, who are not close friends of the offender and have not yet made any significant progress in changing their attitudes, may benefit from their participation in the haircut by being reinforced in their efforts to avoid similar mistakes.

Half-a-dozen haircuts are given out almost every day in Daytop. Sometimes one haircut may be shared by a whole department if its members have fallen down badly in their work—for example, if the kitchen has burned a meal or if the service crew has failed to clean the director's office adequately. At certain times when discipline in the house is becoming relatively loose, haircuts are flying thick and fast. For example, during one such time the person running morning meeting asked everyone who had had a haircut during the past week to raise their hand and half of all those present had their hand raised.

More severe learning experiences are given out much less often. A person may have to wear a large cardboard sign around the neck. This measures about three feet by eighteen inches and carries in large lettering a message pertinent to the individual's problem. It may say, for example, "I am a baby. I cannot control my feelings. Please help me." A sign is deliberately designed to be awkward and to get in a person's way constantly. It makes the performance of many ordinary tasks quite difficult. The purpose of this is to serve as a constant reminder to the person of what he must correct in his behavior and to give him an incentive to demonstrate that he is doing this so that he may earn the reward of being allowed to take off the sign.

Similar thinking lies behind other kinds of learning experience which involve carrying around a symbol of the dereliction which got the person into trouble. For example, someone who persistently forgot to turn off lights was required to carry around a lightbulb at all times and hold it at shoulder height. On another occasion, someone who persistently forgot to check in and out of the building was required to sit on a high stool by the check-in board and shout through a megaphone every time a person entered or left the house, "Don't forget to check in" or "Don't forget to check out." Learning experiences of this kind serve a dual function: as well as helping the individual to learn something, they also serve as constant reminders to the rest of the residents to avoid the same pitfalls. So the deviant individual is in a very real sense performing a useful service to his fellows.

Perhaps the most severe form of learning experience, applied only to male residents, is the *shaved head*. For females the equivalent sanction is to be made to wear a stocking cap which covers all the hair, while they are forbidden to wear makeup. A shaved head is normally given to a resident who splits from the house and then seeks to return. It entails the most severe loss of status, including the loss of all privileges as well as the loss of any job status that the resident may have had. Along with the bald head or stocking cap, a person is normally sent into the "dish-pan," which means that he spends all of his time cleaning pots and utensils in the kitchen or onto "spare parts" which means that he is at the disposal of any senior resident and will be given a series of heavy, monotonous tasks and required to work until late at night.

A shaved head or stocking cap is a treatment reserved for residents who show a deeply-ingrained resistance to the efforts of people in Daytop to teach them new ways of behavior. As one resident who had experienced this sanction personally expressed it, "A bald head tatooes it in your belly." It seems that the combined experience of the shock to one's physical image, the dramatic stripping of status and the long hours of monotonous work combine to make a person take a good look at "where he is at"—the way he has been acting and how he needs to change if he is ever to stay off drugs. Surprisingly, perhaps, residents do put up with this kind of treatment, partly because they fear to run away and partly because they do realize that it is for their own good and because they sense the concern on the part of fellow residents to help them mend their ways and achieve what they came to Daytop for.

Although this most galling of all learning experiences involves stripping a person of all outward vestiges of status, it does not mean that he becomes a pariah or out-cast. He is still a member of the group; his fellows still speak to him, though most of their conversation centers around the difficulties he has found himself in and how he is dealing with them. He is given every assistance in winning back his former status in the group. In the same way that the physical sufferings of the new resident undergoing drug withdrawal are alleviated by the comfort of being accepted as a member of the group, so we find that the harrowing experience of having a shaved head and the accompanying indignities are also mitigated by the help and concern of one's peers. This does not mean, however, that everyone will encourage him to feel sorry for himself, for this is definitely taboo. He is considered to need and deserve the position he is in because of his failings. In a curious way residents sometimes feel more concern when they have a shaved head or a stocking cap than ever before and end up feeling more "part of the house" than ever before.

A former resident and staff member describes what a person goes through when getting a severe learning experience and what they should gain from it.

> First of all, we know that a person who has been using drugs for any amount of time is usually the type of person that does a lot of testing. He'll test and test until somebody stops him. So the learning experience will be a shot of reality like you've never had before. It'll stop him right in his tracks. So the concept of it is to stop whatever negatively is going on so that he can take a look at it. The kind of things that a person goes through in that situation are usually the things that he has never wanted to look at or maybe never has looked at. They are: number one, that he's been caught; two, that he's looking bad in his own eyes and he's looking bad to his peers; number three, he has to make a decision—he

> knows that he can no longer do that here, so if he wants to continue to do it, he's gonna have to leave; if he wants to stay, he's gonna have to work on it and change it. Because of the situation that's been set up, those are usually the immediate changes he's gonna go through. Either he's gonna become open and accept it, or he's gonna become defensive and say "No, it's not me. It's an injustice," and split. I think that's the first set of feelings that he experiences.
>
> The person who stays—let's take an example at random—if he's wearing a sign, he walks out of the office, and he feels like a real schmuck. He's got this big piece of cardboard hanging around his neck saying "I am a stupid idiot. I steal cigarettes when nobody's looking. Please help me." He knows he's gonna have to go around to 25 residents and explain to each one what happened. He's really gonna feel inadequate because his image of a man is no longer gonna support him in this situation. The feelings he's gonna go through are ones of feeling inadequate and feeling in many cases like he doesn't know whether he can handle it or not. This is where the support of the environment is gonna be very important. Unless he gets the proper support at that time that guy will probably split—unless he's a really strong guy.

It may well seem to the reader that the community we are describing is inhumane and its leaders sadistic. It must be remembered, however, that Daytop Village was created and exists in order to help drug addicts to change their way of life and become able to live without drugs. Daytop residents are here because they say they want to achieve this. A few are able to learn to make the changes necessary in themselves with no learning experiences more severe than a haircut every once in a while. But such individuals are rare. A great majority of confirmed drug addicts became addicts because of weaknesses in their character, and the lives they led as addicts served only to exaggerate and confirm these character weaknesses. Even when they find themselves in a place like Daytop, therefore, with all the group support and pressure toward certain kinds of behavior, it is still impossible for many residents to conform consistently to these norms. Drastic measures are used only because more gentle ones are ineffective. If it is hard to accept that some people have the right to impose such harsh sanctions on others, what should they then do? Throw them out? Or allow them to remain in Daytop, sabotaging the efforts of those who might benefit more from the community?

Our description of learning experiences or negative sanctions has been far lengthier than our account of positive sanctions. To some extent this reflects the fact that there are simply more negative sanctions; it also suggests the fact that in Daytop there is less emphasis on rewarding good behavior in formal ways and more emphasis on correcting bad behavior. This is a system that has been evolved in Synanon and found to be effective both there and in Daytop. Daytop leaders do try to provide some theoretical justification for it by saying:

> Why should we reward you for acting responsibly and not shooting dope? That's what you're supposed to do. It's what most people out there are doing anyway. We're not going to give you a medal for it. That's just what it means to be a normal decent human being."

We should not overlook, though, a most important source of positive rewards to Daytop residents as they achieve some consistency in their new patterns of responsible behavior. This is the feeling of gratification that the resident gets from personal achievement. Along with this inner reward and outweighing it much of the time is the social reward of finding that he is rising in the estimation of fellow residents. He also finds that as he makes a greater effort to show concern for fellow residents, as the norms require, they in turn demonstrate concern for him. When he is doing well in terms of Daytop standards, he feels an increase of approval and respect from his fellows and, conversely, when he is failing he senses disappointment from them. The people from whom he receives these sentiments are people who have a unique importance to him. Outside of Daytop, most residents have no valid human contacts—commonly their families have rejected them for their persistent lies and stealing; they become aware that most of those who seemed to be their friends "on the street" were only companions of convenience; and to most of society they are considered dangerous vermin. Here in Daytop, though, they are learning the meaning of concern, friendship, and trust. It becomes important to them to live up to these new standards of morality. To fail in Daytop becomes not just a matter of incurring negative sanctions from the directorship but a matter of letting down people who have shown trust and tried to help. It also gradually becomes a matter of letting oneself down. However, these more noble forms of sanction are slow to develop and for a long time much of the control of residents' behavior at Daytop rests heavily on the positive and negative sanctions we have described.

AUTHORITY IN DAYTOP

Residents in Daytop have nearly all had serious problems in accepting authority —either they have overtly flouted authority or they have accepted it on the surface only to "thumb their nose" at it privately. In some cases the very act of shooting dope can be seen in this light. Neither staff nor other leading residents will, in fact, spend any significant amount of time trying to analyze with residents the psychological origins of their drug addiction in terms of their attitude to authority. They will merely point out to residents who have a problem in either accepting orders or in accepting the person who must give them orders *as a person* (rather than just as an oppressive authority figure) that their behavior is falling into this particular pattern and that they had better work on it. That is, they had better try harder to conform to the norms and to work on getting to the root of the feelings that underlie this problem. (In Chapters 5 and 6, we shall discuss the ways provided for dealing with feelings of this kind.)

As observers with a sociological perspective, we may note certain important features of the authority structure of Daytop. In the first place, to make the point in its most unsophisticated form—as the resident is likely to perceive it—the kinds of people who have authority over the new Daytop residents are different from the kinds of people he is accustomed to having in positions of authority over him. The occupants of authority positions in secular American society tend to be middle-aged (hence considerably older than he), conventionally middle-class in manners, white (highly salient to the black person), and apparently holding their position because of seniority, kinship, or some other political or nonfunctional reason. In

Daytop, by contrast, the new resident's department head and others who give him orders are likely to be little different from him in age, not at all middle-class in manners—even when their social class background was middle-class, and holding the position because they have earned it by their performance in lower positions. Thus the conventional factors that tend to aggravate authority relationships outside of Daytop (age difference, social class mannerisms, and the issue of the supervisor's competence) do not in general apply in Daytop and cannot, therefore, be used by the resident to excuse his failure to accept the authority of those above him.

The factor of race or color cuts either way, according to the race or color of the resident in question. The black or Puerto Rican resident is likely to have a boss of the same ethnic group at some time. If he has a problem in accepting the authority this person and others of different ethnic background, his attitude is revealed for what it is—a problem in accepting authority *per se*. At the same time, learning to accept a boss of a different ethnic group is deemed important for all. It is equally important for the white resident to learn to accept the authority of a black or Puerto Rican boss as it is for the minority ethnic group resident to accept the authority of a white. The same applies to men who have problems in accepting the authority of a female and vice versa. In all cases both superior and subordinate should learn to deal in an objective and honest manner with the grievances they have against each other, in light of the responsibilities assigned to each by the Daytop structure. In front of a jury of their fellow residents, in the encounter group, such grievances can be dealt with. There the complainants get a diagnosis of the problem and a demonstration of what must be done to alleviate it. They may be shown that their perceptions are prejudiced, that they are unable to see the other as a person, that they have not empathized with the demands of the other's social role because of the authority problem.

Another aspect of the typical Daytop resident's problem with authority concerns his attitude toward psychiatrists and other professionals. Typically he does not trust them; he fears and yet despises them because he finds them so easy to deceive and manipulate. The Daytop staff who try to help him, who give him a diagnosis of his problems and tell him what to do are quite different. They speak the same language as the resident, they have had similar experiences; not uncommonly they have "hung out" at the same places and known the same people "on the street," but most important of all the Daytop staff member has personally been through the very same difficulties as the resident to whom he is offering advice and encouragement. He offers medicine that he has already taken himself; he prescribes efforts and changes that he has already made himself and perhaps is still making. All of these factors make the authority more acceptable to the former addict in Daytop.

The longer a resident stays in Daytop, the more likely he is to develop a personal relationship with at least one staff member—one whom he selects as his personal "role model." In long talks the junior resident expresses his problems as well as he can (perhaps quite inarticulately) and the more senior one "identifies" with him. That is, he talks about similar situations in which he has found himself, and describes how he felt. As the newer resident listens and hears the other describe the same feelings that he had but was hardly even aware of, and that he has probably never heard *anyone* talk about previously, a strong feeling of trust develops. He feels concern from the older resident. The two start to know each other as individuals as a result of these conversations. This means that, in this relationship at least, the barrier of authority is slowly broken down. Not only do they overcome the "authority factor" as an obstacle preventing the newer resident from getting to know and understand the senior one, but the latter now starts to have a definite influence over the newer resident, who wants to emulate his "role model" and make him proud of his protégé. What is taking place may be likened in some respects to psychoanalytic transference.

This relationship alone is not enough to explain the effectiveness of the social controls in Daytop. The relationship is slow to mature; and it may only develop with one senior resident. Other mechanisms bolstering conformity are clearly necessary, and these have already been outlined. What remains to be emphasized about these sanctions is that to a very large extent they are administered through a ritual that involves not just one but several residents acting with the authority of Daytop. Hence at each juncture where a Daytop resident has violated a norm and so challenged the authority structure of the house the consequences are meted out to him in a situation where he is out-numbered. This helps the person who is speaking for the Daytop authority structure to speak with assurance that he is in complete control of the situation, and it helps to psychologically overwhelm the person receiving the sanction. If he is tempted to "react" (talk back impolitely) or even to respond with physical violence, those who represent the authority of the group can, by virtue of their great number, keep the upper hand. It should be emphasized that this kind of resistance is an *extremely* rare event in Daytop. This perhaps is due to the psychological effect of staging the administration of formal sanctions either publicly or with the active participation of several residents.

Finally, we must remember the context and circumstances in which a person petitions for acceptance in the Daytop community. Acceptance is at the discretion of the staff and continued residence is contingent on some degree of effort on the part of the individual. Daytop is not obliged to keep any resident and does (though rarely) formally expel anyone who is very uncooperative or who breaks one of the cardinal rules against drugs and violence. Everyone who is accepted as a resident has said before witnesses that he needs help and wants to enter Daytop, and that he agrees to accept the Daytop rules. This gives the staff a clear mandate to exercise their authority over residents. In practice, the latter are forced to put up with this less by the logic of this social contract than by the fear of what faces them on the outside should they split. This may be a jail sentence, or the fear of facing the daily struggle for survival as a junkie again. Although this in itself does nothing to modify the former addict's attitudes to authority, it does tend to keep him in Daytop long enough for the other factors mentioned to have a chance to influence him. Also helping to tilt the balance in favor of staying are the positive experiences that he is beginning to have as a Daytop resident—the security, the sense of having a direction and purpose, the warmth and concern shared with peers.

"TIGHT HOUSE"

So far, our description and analysis of social control in Daytop has been limited to the situation prevailing at the time of this study (1967 and 1968). We have said nothing about the difficult struggle to get the group to that level of functioning. The historical data we have are fragmentary, based on the recollections of a few individuals who lived through the early days and eventually became staff members. This information does, however, add an important new dimension to our understanding of social control in a group such as this.

Before the arrival of David Deitch at Daytop Lodge none of the directors who were hired had any experience at running a drug-free community of former addicts. In other words, none had Synanon experience. In its first year control was very loose at Daytop Lodge. Many residents were allowed to take jobs outside the house, hence they had both the money and the opportunity to buy drugs and alcohol and to smuggle it back into the house. Even at this time, though, Daytop Lodge, in the words of one who was a resident at that time, "was no 'shooting gallery.'" The use of alcohol and drugs was not flagrant, though everyone knew about it and was more or less involved in it. Some discretion was preserved in the manner of consumption, if for no other reason than all residents at this time were on probation and could be easily sent to jail by their probation officers. So each resident helped to cover up for his peers. At this stage, the culture of the Lodge was essentially the same as that of many other well-intentioned but weakly administered projects designed to rehabilitate drug addicts.

The arrival of Deitch changed all of this quite abruptly. He arrived at the Lodge unannounced, his identity unknown to the residents. He took advantage of this temporary anonymity to find out who were some of the violators of the no-drug or alcohol rule. Soon, he made himself known to the residents and called an extraordinary meeting of the whole house in which he made clear his determination that Daytop was going to be a group of people who were committed to *changing* their way of life and learning to live completely without drugs from that point on. He emphasized the importance of honesty and "copping to" one's faults and mistakes. He called for residents to admit to getting high in the house. He confronted some individuals and when some of them copped to something, challenged them to confront others in the house. Those residents who were slow to speak up were therefore confronted by their peers who knew what they had been doing.

Residents also heard their new director demanding that most of those who copped to violations of the cardinal rule, mostly by "getting high," and who wanted to stay in the house, would have to agree to having their heads shaved. A few who spoke up first to confess what they had been doing and to confront their peers were allowed to stay without taking a bald head. Deitch made it clear that anyone who did not want to stay on his terms would be returned to court immediately. He played on the fact that residents had heavy sentences to serve if they were reported to be in violation of the terms of their probation orders, which stipulated that they must remain in treatment at Daytop Lodge.

Faced with this harsh choice, most or all (recollections are not clear on this point) residents accepted Deitch's terms. The house was full of bald heads and the new director had made his point—that he intended to enforce the rules because he took the declared aims of Daytop Lodge absolutely seriously. The point was not just that he was able to command respect and perhaps fear from residents after this incident but that a clean start had been made in establishing a group with norms that were now (on an official level, at least) hostile to drug use and favorable to honesty, concern, and responsibility. In order to instill these qualities in this collection of junkies on probation, the practice of confrontation had to be started for the first time. This actually started in the house meeting and "cop-out" session.

David Deitch, with his years of Synanon experience, his personal example of having given up drugs after many years' addiction, and his dedicated, brilliant leadership, made sure that from that point on the pressure stayed on in Daytop—above all, the pressure to confront each other. A "negative" culture had previously been allowed to develop, with the "inmate *versus* staff" attitude and the "no squealing" code of inmate solidarity that characterizes nearly all of the established and unsuccessful institutions of correction or rehabilitation for addicts or other offenders. It is important to keep this in mind when analyzing Daytop in order to appreciate just how unusual it was after Deitch arrived and for several years thereafter. More recently there have been many replications of the Daytop model in successor communities, many of them founded by ex-Daytop staff. One may be tempted to ask the question: how does Daytop keep functioning with such a high level of social control and avoid slipping back into the negative culture that it once had?

Even now, Daytop occasionally experiences a slackening of discipline and purposefulness among residents. This tends to happen every few months and it is one of a house director's most important functions to be alert to this development and to take steps to reverse the trend. The institutionalized means for doing this is by declaring a "tight house."

This is usually initiated by the calling of a house meeting for everyone in the living room. As soon as this is announced, either by the P.A. system or by expediters coming around to every room or both, everyone becomes "uptight," knowing that something serious is happening but not knowing what it is. When the directors enter there is a greater hush than usual. Usually they keep everyone waiting for not less than twenty minutes. As residents wait, there is no joking and talk is in low whispers.

Sometimes the house director alone will conduct the meeting. Usually he will be accompanied by his immediate colleagues, the assistant director and senior coordinator. If there are co-directors, both will usually share the meeting and in other cases the director commonly turns it over to his colleagues later for them to elaborate. When a "tight house" is to be inaugurated it may or may not be labeled as such. Commonly, though, the director will begin by saying that the house has become very "loose," that the people are "letting things slide." He will give examples of some recent incidents of neglect and carelessness. "People have forgotten what they're here for. They think this is a fucking country club." Sometimes the coordinators may be included in the general indictment but not usually.

The director will talk about the need to "get rid of the deadwood" in the house, the people who are not making any real investment in Daytop and who, consequently, are getting nothing for themselves and dragging everyone else down.

"People will split during the tight house, the people who shouldn't be here anyway because their poor little bellies can't take it. They can't get a look at where they're at and start changing." This is the gist of what is usually said. Usually, too, there is talk of throwing some people out. Sometimes, in order to dramatize this possibility, expediters will be told to start up the vehicles and the sound of motors starting up and running can be heard by everyone in the house meeting. This scares people severely and leads some to start "copping to things" they have been doing wrong or failing to do, when inevitably the "cop-out session" begins.

During the tight house many privileges are revoked, such as phone calls, movie trips, sports, music, and TV. No visitors are allowed in the house and Open House is, of course, cancelled. Most of the residents who have any status lose it until they earn it back again. Typically this will mean that coordinators assume direct charge of their departments while department heads, ramrods, and others holding minor status positions lose them. The house director and his immediate subordinates take over the daily running of the house, in place of the coordinators, for a few days. Higher status departments are reduced to skeleton staffs consisting of the most senior members and the other workers in community relations, expediting, and communications are demoted to service crew and kitchen staff. SPAN staff may be pulled back into the house to help run it if coordinators are also demoted but not as a general rule.

During a tight house the idea is to get back to "basics." To emphasize this a major work project is instituted which begins with GI-ing the whole house and continues with painting some large area or some similar, large-scale project. "Basics" at Daytop center less on work itself than on the way people conduct themselves while working with others. Residents are told that they are expected to be especially diligent at confronting and challenging each other. Feelings run high at this time: there is resentment at loss of privileges and status, fear of not getting them back, and anger and annoyance at many small incidents in the new, extra-stressful situation.

Residents are told not to count on getting their old jobs back. Everything is in the melting pot now. Those who shine will get the vacant positions and statuses. Each day a few more residents are raised up from the mass and either restored to the jobs they had before, to a similar one, or given their first opportunity at holding a position with some status. The appointment of newer residents to coveted statuses increases the panic among those who were formerly occupants of positions on that level and raises the hopes of the newer residents.

Encounter groups may be held every day during a tight house not only to deal with the feelings that are produced but also to give more opportunity for residents to challenge and be challenged about "where they are at," how hard they are really trying to change, and what games and deceptions they continue to play in Daytop. Thus there is extra pressure on residents to "cop to guilt" they are holding onto. These confessions may lead to learning experiences being given to residents to encourage them to "clean up their mess."

Other learning experiences are given for the same kinds of mistakes that would normally earn them, except that the scale of severity is now stepped up. "Signs" are especially favored by the directorship during tight house. They have the advantages of being both very conspicuous for others to see and instantly removable when the staff so decide (unlike the shaved head). During the height of a tight house there may be ten people wearing signs, when only one or two would be seen in more normal times.

One of the declared purposes of the tight house is to "clear out some of the deadwood," residents who are not serious enough about wanting to be in Daytop, who are not making enough effort and are therefore endangering others by their lack of concern. The bare fact that life in the house has now become so much more stressful leads some residents to split. But this is not the only factor operating at this time to increase a desire to leave. The amount of challenging and confronting that goes on during the tight house increases the pressure on residents who are holding onto "guilt." They may split rather than confess and take the consequences.

Then again, during a tight house the staff will tell certain residents to sit on the "prospect chair" and think about whether they want to stay in Daytop. This is the same chair on which prospects seeking admission and residents who think that they want to split are made to sit. The difference here is that the initiative comes, not from the resident, but from the staff, who pick out residents who seem to them to be especially low in motivation to stay. The prospect chair symbolizes the boundary between Daytop and the outside, so that a person sitting on it is halfway in and halfway out of Daytop. This experience is designed to help the resident really focus his mind on deciding how much he wants to stay in Daytop.

He can now sit on the fence no longer; he must jump one way or the other. However, if he opts to stay in Daytop, there is no automatic acceptance. Usually he must "reinvest" to prove his sincerity. The nature of the reinvestment may take many forms. Some common ones are for him to have to ask a general meeting of the house to reaccept him and submit to their challenging questions or to have a shaved head. Otherwise it would be too easy for him to merely say he wanted to stay and put off the real decision until he got into the next situation of pressure and then split. The point, though, is to find out *now* who is deadwood and get rid of them *now*, in order for the group atmosphere to be recharged with the unanimity of purpose that is necessary for success.

The Daytop community can be likened to a group of castaways on the open sea. If they all paddle very hard in the right direction they can all get to safety and dry land. They know in which direction they must go but some of them are easily distracted from paddling and some like to fool around in ways which actively impede those who are trying to paddle consistently. The problem is clear. No one member of this group can save himself alone. Together, as a group they can all save themselves—but only if they either persuade the nonconformists to cooperate or get rid of them. The choice is stark but inescapable. This is the purpose of the tight house and also the purpose of most features of the social control system of Daytop which we have described.

5 / Encounter groups

PRELIMINARIES

Daytop comprises a complex therapeutic environment in which virtually everything that happens to a resident may have a particular therapeutic value. Within this total environment there are various recognized therapeutic "tools" which are considered to have a special importance—such as pull-ups, haircuts, seminars, and morning meetings. Although we have just discussed a number of these practices as tools of social control, it must be understood that they serve equally as tools of personal growth. Learning to conform to group norms and exercise impulse control is therapeutically important for the individual resident as well as being important for social control; participating in the enforcement of rules similarly has a dual function, as does learning to show concern and to play helping roles within Daytop. Included in the list of the basic "tools of the environment" are groups.

On Wednesday nights all residents meet in "static groups," the same eight to ten persons coming together every week at this time. On Mondays and Fridays everyone takes part in "encounter groups" in which residents who have problems with certain other residents are brought together.

Thus on encounter nights no one knows in advance which group he will be in—or with whom. Shortly before it is time for encounters, the whole house gathers in the living room. The atmosphere is tense; many residents are very nervous. Yet there is a particular feeling of excitement that is present at no other time. There are many reasons for this. Those who have done something to anger someone else know that they will probably be the target of loud and angry abuse and then quite likely will be hauled over the coals by the whole group. Those who have grievances against others may be afraid of yelling but know that they are expected to do so and are anxious to get it over with; also they may be worried about having the complaint "turned around on them" so that it is made to seem like their own fault. Some residents, once they have gotten their bearings in Daytop, come to find participation in groups exciting and gratifying. (At Synanon encounter groups are called "games".) From the outsider's perspective, though, what stands out is the relentless scrutiny of the group into each other's conduct and progress, the merciless spotlighting of faults and the insistent demands for definite and specific commitments to change that conduct.

A hush falls on the throng in the living room when the "guru" appears, carrying his lists of names. This person is a staff member on coordinator level who has the job of counseling distressed residents who want to talk with him, teaching the philosophy of the house in its widest sense to residents, and making up encounter groups to bring together as many of the residents who have business with each other as possible.

The mechanics for setting up encounter groups are basically simple, though the number of different possible combinations out of eighty-odd residents is enormous. A resident who has business with a fellow resident that he wants to bring up in groups "drops a slip" on that person, by writing on a slip of paper his (the complainant's) name, the name of the accused, and a very brief statement of the nature of the complaint. This slip is deposited in the encounter box. Shortly before it is time for groups the guru empties these slips out and proceeds to sort them out. On an average encounter group night there will be somewhere between twenty and thirty slips in the encounter box.

The encounter box or "slip box" is one of the first things a new resident learns on entering Daytop. He learns that he may not "react" to another resident by arguing or expressing resentment. He must "stuff" these feelings for now and "drop a slip" so that he can deal with them in the only approved way—in the groups.

Although there are some differences between static groups and encounter groups in the way they operate, these differences are minor compared to their common features. For simplicity we shall discuss mainly their common features here and use the term "enounter groups" to cover static groups as well. Later we shall comment briefly on the differences between them.

Two main functions are served by Daytop groups: first, they provide a legitimate and carefully regulated outlet for verbal hostility and aggression which the strict rules of the house do not permit to be released at any other time; second, groups are the setting for intense "reality therapy" in which a person is forced to listen to others telling him how they see him behaving, pointing out how certain problems that he is complaining about are the result of his own behavior, and confronting him about how he feels about himself.

Each group generally consists of eight to twelve members, representing a cross section of the house in terms of Daytop experience. Chairs are arranged in a circle and each group is far enough away from other groups so that no one need worry about making too much noise. In any case, the taboo on swearing and shouting that applies most of the time in Daytop is lifted during groups. No one is allowed to leave his seat, though, and no one is allowed to threaten another person or throw anything.

GROUPS IN SESSION

The usual way for encounter groups to start is for someone, usually one of the senior members present, to say "Are there any slips in this group?" There may be a pause, then someone will scream a torrent of loud and angry abuse at another member of the group. The latter may reply in kind or he may refrain from doing so, scorning the indictment. Typically, the person letting out his angry feelings does so at ear-splitting volume and in the earthiest of language.

The rhetoric for expressing hostile and angry feelings in Daytop groups is quite standardized as to vocabulary and imagery. A typical confrontation goes like this:

> Listen, motherfucker, you'd better quit messing with me. 'Cos I don't take that shit from no one, see? So just knock off that shit. I don't like it. I don't fucking like it and I don't have to take that fucking shit from you, cocksucker.

The emphasis at this point is on expressing the sheer, gut-level intensity of the feelings involved—"dumping the garbage" that has built up from the strains of trying to live up to the exacting standards of conduct and work imposed here—getting haircuts, having to take orders and never being allowed to react, protest or let out one's feelings of anger and resentment.

The torrent of noise and anger subsides and someone asks "What happened?" or "What is that all about?" The one who dropped the slip and dumped his garbage in the group, as he is supposed to, is now supposed to give a calm and objective account of what the other person did to make him so angry. Other members of the group act as cross-examiners and jury, probing to get at the truth and limiting any further expression of anger now that the legitimate outlet has just been used.

Perhaps A is accusing B of picking on him by repeatedly choosing him for extra duties while he passes over others. B will be confronted directly by group members as to whether he does this. This may not be the first time that such an indictment has been made and proven against him. In any event he may "cop to it" fairly readily.

Then again, B may start out by denying the charge and attempt to "turn it around" on A by claiming that he is lazy and always has a bad attitude to work in the house. Which way things develop from here depends on the leader of the group. Tacitly, the resident with most status in the house—either a coordinator or a department head with seniority—acts as group leader. He or she will decide, on the basis of what has emerged in the group and what he already knows about A and B which of them is most at fault. If he feels it is mostly B, he will press the indictment and continue to confront him with increasing pressure. The other active members of the group will follow suit and support this move. If, on the other hand, he feels that A has no valid indictment but just a load of garbage to dump because of the normal difficulties of adjusting to life in Daytop, then the indictment will be "turned around" on A. Again the leader normally makes this decision and the rest of the group follows.

So long as the person being confronted refuses to admit that he is wrong, the pressure from the group continues and builds up. Other members of the group throw in his face previous incidents that reflect the same pattern he is denying now; someone in the group may have witnessed the actual incident that gave rise to the present complaint and if he feels that the indictment is valid he will throw his weight as an impartial eyewitness into the balance. Most telling of all, perhaps, is when someone "pulls his cover" by revealing something said to him in private by the person being confronted that contradicts the position he is publicly maintaining.

If the person being confronted remains stubborn, it will be pointed out to him that everyone in the group is unanimous in the way they perceive him, while he maintains the contrary. Then he will very likely be told:

> We have a saying around here that says: If one person tells you you're a horse, he is probably crazy; if two people tell you, maybe they're both crazy; but if the whole group tells you you're a horse, you'd better go out and buy a saddle.

Let us assume that the group is confronting A and that he admits that his original grievance is invalid. He will then be confronted about the need to change his lazy attitude and get involved in the house. At this point someone will typically say this:

> If you don't change that attitude you'll do what I did and split in no time at all. Then you'll have to take a bald head to get back in—that's if you don't OD (overdose) or get yourself locked up in jail before that. So why don't you dig where things are at and give this place a chance. Sure it's hard but wasn't it awful hard out on the street too? And when you start to make some friends in here—real friends—then you'll really see that it's worth it. Why don't you give it a try?

A will probably agree to this but he will be pushed to give a further token of his sincerity. He will usually be asked to "make a commitment" to the group. This will be a promise to start making some specific changes in his behavior right away, regardless of the fact that it is hard. He has been asked to "give the house a try" and to change his attitude. This is important but it is a long-term process and it is hard to tell whether he is really doing it until much later. With a specific behavioral commitment, for example, to talk to more people about himself, to make himself heard in morning meeting, or to make more pull-ups around the house, there are clear criteria as to whether or not he is keeping the commitment. Fulfilling the terms of such a specific commitment can legitimately be taken as a demonstration of his sincerity about the broader undertaking to change his attitude—and failing to keep the specific one clearly indicates a failure in the wider one.

The commitment, when made, is apt to be remembered by fellow-members in the group who will throw it back in his face if he fails to keep it. The embarrassment of this is great and is keenly felt by residents who might suffer no guilt feelings from failing to keep a promise. When A accepts his commitment that is usually the end of his turn on the "hot seat." (This term was not heard in Daytop but is used here for brevity.)

As an alternative to the scenario we have just outlined, the group might have focused on B, the object of the original indictment. He may admit that he was, in fact, picking on A for more than his share of extra work. In that case the group will now focus on him. Why does he pick only "easy shots" for clean-ups and other extra duties? Why does he regard A as an easy shot? Shouldn't he be showing A some concern instead of taking advantage of him? How does he feel about himself, knowing that he is scared to pick the more self-assured or aggressive residents and only picks ones who are too new or too frightened to intimidate him?

The group will encourage B to talk about his feelings of inadequacy about himself, which generally lie at the bottom of such behavior and about how threatened and insecure he feels about his position in the house. Others in the group, especially

An encounter group in session. These photos were taken at Marathon House in Coventry, Rhode Island. Although this group took place several years after the fieldwork on which the text is based and in another location, the group process does not differ significantly. Photographs by Marvin Coe.

the older ones, will "identify" with him and tell how they have felt very similar feelings. But, they point out to him, this is no way to feel better about himself—by abusing his authority over others. Insofar as his bad feelings about himself are based on the way he feels that others regard him, he will be encouraged to con-

front these people, beginning right in the group and continuing later "on the floor." When he does this he will sometimes find that others see him in a more favorable light than he thought; sometimes he will find that his fellows do indeed perceive him unfavorably because they dislike certain things that he does, thus presenting him with the choice of either changing that behavior or learning to live with the disapproval. If B says that he knows what he should do, he will probably be asked to make a specific commitment to do it.

In any event, whichever of them is felt to be the more at fault, the group generally has something to say to the other. Whether the group concentrates on A or B as the main target, they will usually have something to say to the other party, for he usually has contributed to the problem in some way. This sharing of the blame tends to make the person who takes the main brunt of it feel a little less aggrieved, but there is no avoiding the fact that someone who has received a heavy confrontation and criticism in his group is going to feel bad about it. Members of the group attempt to "patch him up" during the group itself and immediately afterward, by expressing confidence in his ability to make the necessary changes, by identifying from personal experience and describing how they themselves have been in a similar situation and came through it successfully, and by trying to make it clear that they still accept him as a person and as a friend even though they reject and disapprove of certain aspects of his behavior.

We have just analyzed the way one indictment in encounter groups may develop, considering two alternative possibilities: it may be turned around on him or the group may back him up in pressing it home on the other party. It is important for Daytop residents to get this group feedback and to be forced to realize how other people see them acting and how other people feel about their behavior, for drug addicts are notoriously prone to acting selfishly and "coming off their bellies" (responding on the basis of their immature feelings) while closing their eyes to how much they hurt other people by doing this. So the group forces them to look at the reality of how they act, and it puts pressure on them to change their behavior. It also tries to get them to look at "what is happening" with them, and causing them to act the way they do. This is the second and more difficult phase of the encounter group process.

All the transactions in groups do not follow this pattern of indictment and investigation. Much of the time in encounter groups—though not all—is occupied in this way, but static groups do not usually operate this way. The other most common form of transaction in groups is for one person present to be asked "What's happening?" He is then expected to talk about how he has been feeling lately and what "changes" (difficult transitions) he has been going through. In the static groups the entire session will typically be spent by those present taking turns relating in this fashion.

"Relating" in this way in groups is less tightly patterned than relating to specific grievances, hence it imposes more of a burden of responsibility both on the person relating and on the other members of the group to get beyond the superficial matters and the glib complacency that come most easily to a person's lips when he or she is asked "What's happening?" Sometimes the response to this question is a sullen "Nothing" or "I don't know." This may come from a new resident who is resenting the new restrictions and demands which he suddenly finds placed upon him or from an older resident who is temporarily going through a difficult period. It is unlikely that anyone maintaining such an attitude could survive for long in Daytop. The constant confrontations and the learning experiences which he would bring upon himself would most likely soon lead him to either change his attitude or split. But, equally, there are few Daytop residents who do not go through phases like this at some time or other. The following example shows how an unresponsive new resident may be handled in groups. It also provides an illustration of how one resident may "pull the covers" of another.

BILL: "What's with you, Joe?"
JOE: "Nothing." (He shrugs.)
BILL: "You haven't said a thing in the whole group."
JOE: "Got nothing to say."
RAY: "He doesn't open his mouth all day."
BILL: "Nothing's bothering you?"
JOE: "No."
RAY: "He's still playing sick."

Several people taunt him about this.

BILL: "You stuffing, Joe?" [Shirking work and avoiding involvement.]
JOE: "Sure I'm stuffing."
BILL: "How come you've got nothing to say?"
JOE: "I got nothing to say."
FRANK: "I knew you on the street and in the joint [jail], Joe, and you always had plenty to say. You had a real big mouth."
BILL: "What happened to that tough guy image, Joe?"

Bill goes on to talk about how he himself cultivated a tough guy image on the street, like so many others, talking tough out of the side of his mouth "when all the time I was scared shit." In here, he explains, no one looks up to a person for being a tough guy; here we are trying to be honest. People do not succeed all the time but when they slip into lies, they are liable to have their covers pulled.

Bill uses the expression "act as if," which Joe reacts to angrily as he does not understand it. Bill explains it, then tells him:

"You should be going up to people and saying 'Hey man, what does this mean? Explain this to me!' When you spoke in the meeting this morning, didn't you feel better afterwards?"
"Yes."

Ideally each group member will have his or her turn to be the focus of the group's attention in the course of each session—usually with the exception of the leader who will mostly deal with his problems in special groups for coordinators. Everyone in the group is also expected to contribute while others are being talked to—to "show them some concern." Toward the end of the group anyone who has been a nonparticipant will probably be confronted about this. Early in my stay at Daytop I was spoken to about this—after the end of the group. (Perhaps my position as a visitor gained me gentler treatment than a resident would have received, though it certainly did not save me from some fierce attacks in later groups.) "How do you feel about not contributing anything to the group? . . . not showing any concern for those people?" The questions are rhetorical and do not really call for an answer. When I replied in embarrassment that I felt unsure of what to say and did not want to disrupt the dynamics of the group, I was told what I have since heard said to many newcomers to groups, "It doesn't matter what you say at first." The important thing is to show some involvement in what is happening—so that the person under the spotlight will not feel that he is being watched by cold-blooded observers, and so that the person who is getting involved will learn how to lend support to the group in the approved manner.

Any particular member of the group (call him "A") may, at any moment, be one of the people shouting at B for his lack of honesty and then, soon, B's turn may be over and A may be on the receiving end of the group's attentions. There is no clear-cut division between those who give and those who receive treatment, between the sick and the well. This is a therapeutic community where everyone is both a donor and a recipient of therapy; where the validity of an observation is independent of the person making it. Here a group member does not have to be well himself to be capable of giving help. Nor does he have to be ashamed of accepting help from his fellows who may, in some respects, be just as sick as he or sicker.

SOCIAL ROLES IN THE ENCOUNTER GROUP

So far we have analyzed what happens in the group in terms of how an emotional indictment or outburst is transformed into a searching factual investigation of one person's progress—either that of the complainant or the accused—followed usually by a bout of "therapy," in the sense of a deliberate and concerted attempt to modify the individual's behavior on all levels—perceptual, emotional, motivational, and purely behavioral. Now we wish to focus on another aspect of this process, the different helping roles which are commonly played by group members and which tend to bring about these results.

It is possible to isolate ten or more distinct helping roles that are played in the encounter group. One group member may play more than one in the same session. Indeed it would be unusual for one person to play only one type of helping role. At the same time, any particular role or type of role may be played by more than one member of the group. This typology of roles is the creation of the observer; it is not something of which Daytop staff or residents appear to be explicitly aware. Certainly it is not taught to residents, as are so many aspects of Daytop theory.

One role may be labelled "chairman." He or she calls members to order and redirects the focus of attention when, for example, it is time to switch from emotional catharsis to rational discussion, or when the person in the hot seat has succeeded (either through his own astuteness or the carelessness of other group members) in slipping out of the spotlight too soon while the discussion shifts to someone else's conduct, or when it is time to switch the spotlight on to another member.

The "prosecutor" (who may, of course, be the same person as the chairman) presses home an indictment which the accused is unwilling to admit or even consider. Several "prosecutors" may go to work on the same person together.

The "witness" or "informant" comes forward spontaneously to support the prosecutor with personal testimony in the form "I saw you. . . ." "Pulling a person's covers" is a special form of this role. The prosecutor may, of course, be his own witness but the impact is greater where two or more group members take up these roles.

The "identifier" tells about a personal experience of his own which is similar to the situation of the person in the hot seat. This may be used to patch up a person who has been open with the group or to help a person who is unwilling to be open, as in the following example:

> Ed came into the group feeling very angry because he was just refused a request for permission to write home. He has expressed a lot of resentment at the staff and the house in general, claiming that he deserves the letter as he has been "doing what he has to do." All the other residents in the group challenge him: *how long* has he been "doing what he has to do"? "how long ago did he get his bald head? (answer: two weeks) [They are playing the role of "prosecutor."] Ed continues to be angry and hostile. Several group members continue in the role of prosecutor. "You look on this place as another joint (jail)." "You can't relate about yourself. You can't be honest." "When we were working our balls off to build something here . . . you were still sniffing airplane glue out there, dingbat." After this second onslaught, Ed goes quiet. Then, very gently, John who was just shouting at him in the role of prosecutor begins to identify with him. He talks about how he fought the Concept at first, wanted everything to be *his* way, and as a result got hit over the head all the time. Finally, after eight or nine months, he decided to try it their way. He started to relate and be open with people. After a while he could look back and see the change in himself. He began to feel good about himself. Then he would sometimes lie in bed at night and remember how frightened and lonely he used to feel. And he isn't like that any more. "Man, that's a beautiful feeling."

Identifying makes the person who is being spoken to feel more a part of the group and especially close to the one who is identifying. In situations like that of the example just given it tends to make the other person less resistant and hostile and more willing to accept what is being said to him. Other situations in which identifying is especially important are those where a person has spoken very openly about feelings that are very hurtful to him or her—perhaps weeping freely. In such cases identifying is very important for making that person feel that the group is "with" him, empathizing and sharing his feelings.

The "preacher" or "moralizer" tells another person what he must do about changing his behavior and attitude. This role figures largely throughout Daytop—it is played by those who run morning meeting, those who make pull-ups (at any time including morning meeting), and those administering haircuts. It is also seen in groups. "You've got to knock off that lazy attitude of yours." "Listen to what people tell you and quit reacting all over the place." "Come out from the woodwork and make yourself felt a bit around here—let's hear you in morning meeting for a start."

The preacher or moralizer also tries to help the other person strengthen his motivation, for example, painting him a word-picture of what he can look forward to at the end of his present struggles if he persists, contrasted with what he has if he gives up. He can feel good about himself; he can be a good husband and a good father, someone his wife and children can be proud of. He can make up to his parents and friends who tried to help him for all the times he let them down, lied to them, and stole from them.

The "reflector" or "mirror" tells a person how they see him or her, usually as a corrective to the person's own distorted self-perception. Sometimes this takes the direction of encouraging someone who is unduly miserable. In one example where this was observed, Paul volunteers to talk in the group and says how bad he feels about himself. When asked why, he replies that it is because he feels that he is very ugly and because he was a "punk" on the street and was too scared to resist people who attacked him physically. Fellow group members say that they do not see him as being exceptionally ugly, and anyway it does not affect their acceptance of him. They also point out that fleeing from attackers who were bigger than him and out numbered him was the sensible thing to do. To reinforce this point, a couple of the males in the group identify by talking of situations where they have also run from attackers when outmatched and when they have stayed to fight and regretted it. This is how they see his behavior and his appearance.

The "reflector" or "mirror" also operates to break down the illusions of the resident who thinks he is doing nothing wrong and who is in fact mistaken. When a number of fellow group members insist together that a person is (for example) arrogant, it is hard for him to insist that he is not. For "arrogant" refers not to his behavior alone, nor to his intentions, but to the way he "comes across to others." So if they say he comes across as arrogant to them, he has to accept this. That is to say that *logically* he has to accept this, though in practice Daytop residents do sometimes refuse to accept such advice—sometimes openly rejecting it but more often inwardly rejecting it while outwardly agreeing to take a look at it.

The distinction between understanding something in one's head and feeling "in the gut" that it is really true is one that is well appreciated by senior residents in Daytop and is something they try hard to help the others to understand. Hence this theme appears frequently in groups, with leaders saying to a person, "That is what you *think*. What you *feel* in your gut is quite different." Commonly it is the latter (the gut feeling which is not acknowledged) that lies behind destructive behavior which is at first incomprehensible. For example, a resident who considers himself fairly well-educated may *say* that he does not resent working for a department head who is an eighth-grade drop-out in a "white collar" job in Daytop. Yet he persists in making foolish mistakes repeatedly in his work. He may actually *believe* what he says (that he has no resentment) because he is so far out of touch with his gut-level feelings. In the group setting the others may attempt to help him get in touch with his real feelings of resentment, humiliation, and suppressed anger toward his boss, on the assumption that these very natural but repressed feelings have been making him uptight and causing him to make many mistakes. In a case like this the role of the "irritant" can be very valuable in triggering an outburst of the very feelings which the person in the "hot seat" has so strenuously denied. Surprised and relieved to have dumped some of the garbage that was messing him up, he realizes "it was there all the time."

The "irritant" is a role played in groups toward a resident who is felt to be "stuffing his feelings," that is, repressing them instead of letting them out in groups. Feelings of hostility and anger are usually the focus of attention for the irritant. His aim is to aggravate his victim in the group to the point where the latter will explode with verbal rage at him. This will be beneficial for the "victim" if he has previously been unable to release his hostile feelings in this way. Any kind of taunt may be used here. With males, taunts of "pussy" and other such homosexual accusations are the most common ploy of the irritant. When someone in the groups opens up this line of approach, others will often join in, so that the whole group in effect plays irritant.

The role of "therapist" is the most complex of all and hence the hardest to define. When the person who is the focus of the group's attention has been forced to examine his own recent conduct in the house, aided by "prosecutors," "informants," "reflectors," and "identifiers," and when he has been made to relate to the feelings about himself, aided perhaps by irritants and probably by identifiers, what happens then? It may be simply that the moralist chimes in and points out to him what urgent changes in his behavior and outlook he must make. Or the group process may be more elaborate and involve the intervention of someone in the role of "therapist."

The "therapist" offers insights to explain *why* the person who is presently under scrutiny has been acting the way he has. The explanation is, of course, designed to help him change it. Whereas this role figures very prominently in professional counseling and psychiatry, it plays a more minor part in Daytop groups. Where it is found, the therapist's insights are offered usually in relation to current or very recent behavior, not in relation to early childhood memories, and the manner of delivering the insights is altogether different.

The Daytop therapist might point out to someone who has just spoken about feeling lonely and friendless how his own behavior has been keeping people away from him—perhaps people in that very group who have wanted to be friends with him. The therapist will find out if there are in fact others in the group who have tried to be friends with him but have been deterred by his behavior. If they do not speak up spontaneously, the therapist will prompt them to do so. He is cueing them to play the "reflector" role—at least that is part of what he is doing here. Or he will ask the person who has just spoken about having no real friends if there is anyone present in the group with whom he would really like to be friends. He may then encourage him to make some overtures then and there, to at least declare his hopes of friendship to the other person. The therapist may then ask if he is afraid of getting close to some people and having a real friendship. Commonly the answer is "yes." The therapist then suggests that this fear has not only been keeping him from taking the initiative but has even reinforced his unfriendly behavior in order to keep others at a distance.

This example represents a common pattern of behavior in Daytop and the role attributed to the Daytop "therapist" is again typical, though not based on any one recorded incident. It should be noted that the role of the therapist here goes far beyond merely offering insights. He also engineers the group process to reinforce dramatically the points he is making and to motivate the subject to act immediately upon the insight.

The last of the legitimate roles we shall discuss before considering two illegitimate practices, is that of the "patch-up artist." In a successful encounter between an individual and his group, the individual will have been hit hard with some unpalatable truths and may in addition have opened himself up to talk about some very sore and intimate subjects. Such encounters create a very strong tendency on the part of this individual to shrink into himself when it is over and to avoid communication with the others who witnessed and participated in his ordeal. The extent to which other group members identify with him is a very powerful factor in determining how acute his tendency to withdraw from the others will be. The more identification takes place, the less powerful is the desire to withdraw from the other group members. What also helps to overcome this problem is the "patch-up" which is supposed to take place when each person concludes their spell on the "hot seat" and is supposed to continue after the group session is over.

The patch-up conveys several messages, more or less explicitly: (1) we still accept you personally, even though we have condemned some of your behavior; (2) most of us have been where you are right now, so we know that you can come through it successfully and we are not feeling "holier than thou"; (3) we look to you to keep the commitment you have made just now, and, because we care about you, we intend to follow up on you and see that you don't fall down on your promise. These messages are conveyed not only by the words spoken at this juncture but also by the warmth that is projected through facial expressions and other nonverbal media. After groups finish everyone generally drifts into the dining room to get coffee. Then people sit down, usually two together, in the dining room or living room. This is the continuation of the patch-up. Two people who were involved in a dispute are under a special obligation to sit down and talk right after the group.

"Throwing out a bone" is an illegitimate practice that is recognized and so named in Daytop. It refers to the common tendency of those who are under the scrutiny of the group to offer relatively innocuous and painless topics of discussion in place of the things that are really bothering them at the time. In contrast with all of the roles previously discussed, this behavior is practiced by the person *receiving* help. By way of example, someone may offer to talk about his feelings that his department head undervalues his efforts or his frustrations at not being allowed to write home when he should really be talking about his continuing mistrust of people in the house. What constitutes throwing out a bone is, of course, relative to the individual. For someone who had already talked about it a couple of times already, to talk about not trusting anyone would constitute bone-throwing in his case. He should perhaps be talking about how he feels about himself and why he is afraid to trust people.

"Red-crossing" is an illegitimate helping role. It consists of attempting to intervene on someone else's behalf when they are under the spotlight and, for example, saying "what he really means to say is. . . ." This role is quickly spotted and the attempt squelched. Anyone trying it more than once would be sure to get themselves confronted as to "where they were coming from."

THE SOCIAL CONTEXT OF THE ENCOUNTER GROUP

It is impossible to understand the dynamics of the encounter group without taking into account its social context. First, the members, as Daytop residents, are living under acute strain. They have been shaken out of their accustomed role of complete withdrawal and are being required to show unaccustomed levels of awareness, honesty, responsibility, concern, and self-control. As if this were not enough, the policy of Daytop is to give them jobs that are difficult for them and generally to put them in difficult situations, so that they are under additional strain. The encounter serves them as a safety valve for these stresses, and for the feelings to which they give rise. The object of this policy is to train residents to be able to cope with greater amounts and different kinds of uncertainty and stress, building up to the greatest stress of all—leaving Daytop to operate in the outside community.

Second, members of the encounter group work and live together (unlike the members of a more typical therapy group), so that many of the strains in each person's life arise directly out of his daily interaction with the other people in his encounter group. A feels a grievance against B because of the way he thinks B has been treating him; so A cares very much about getting B to see that he has been acting inconsiderately. However, if A is being unfair and merely projecting his own feelings on to B, others in the group will point this out to him. Then a third factor comes into play. In the encounter group there will be members who see A and B but are not involved in grievances against either. They can speak up against A, putting *him* on the stand, either instead of B or alongside him.

The main point here is that the basic material for discussion comes from the *concrete* day-by-day incidents of group life. Unlike the client who is in professional group or individual treatment and spends only a few hours each week with his therapist, Daytop residents live full-time with their therapists and, in a sense, they are each others' therapists. It is not, therefore, among the prime requisites for successful treatment in Daytop that the resident have a highly developed power of abstract and analytical thought (as is the case with many other forms of therapy) in order to imagine connections between far-removed causal factors and his present predicament, for in Daytop one deals primarily with the here-and-now. Nor does the efficacy of treatment in Daytop depend upon each resident being scrupulously honest and responsible by bringing into the group on his own initiative an accurate account of his recent behavior, as treatment outside of a therapeutic community does. It depends simply on his being honest enough to look at what his peers point out to him. It does not depend on the much more sophisticated level of honesty necessary for someone to cop to his own faults without pressure from others.

The last point about the dynamics of the encounter concerns the motivation to participate. Residents cannot walk out or fail to come because attendance is absolutely mandatory and absences are literally unheard of. This much is clear enough; however, they could still stay in the encounter room and "switch off" mentally by using the habits of withdrawal so familiar to them. But this would not be effective either because the norms require participation in, as well as presence at, the encounter groups. The more vigilant members of the group encourage, coax, goad, and bully the silent ones into contributing something—they must both contribute to the exploration of someone else's problems and talk about their own.

In allocating residents to groups, care is taken to spread the newest residents around, so that each one finds himself in an integrated, ongoing group. His presence will tend to stimulate residents who are only a little further advanced than he to act much more committed to Daytop and its values. In this way the latter will be fulfilling what the more senior residents expect of them. There is, in effect, a ladder of social control. To simplify: the most senior residents watch the middle ones and pull them up when they slip; the middle residents (watched by the seniors) watch the new ones. As a result, the group member who, at a particular time, is leading in the questioning and challenging gets a great deal of support from the rest of the group: they reinforce his questions with their own and they help to present united group pressure on the member who is reluctant to look further at his own conduct and character in the terms it is presented to him.

As far as keeping the group orderly, this support is also vital. A united group can curb members who want to rant and rave for too long and are reluctant to get down to an objective discussion of the problem; it also serves to control members who might want to talk out of turn and interject their own problems, instead of helping to sort out the one already begun. Thus the social pressures brought to bear on each resident in encounter groups are vital in making the groups operate effectively. While ensuring conformity with the rules governing the group, they also mobilize a great deal of peer level pressure to make a person reflect on his behavior and commit himself publicly to specific changes right away.

An important aspect of the social context of encounter groups and the whole therapeutic process in Daytop concerns their relationship to the power structure of the Daytop community. We have, so far, taken account of only one side of the power problem—how social control is maintained according to the norms set up by the staff. Daytop is an authoritarian group in which the rules and expectations are determined unilaterally by a small elite group, uninfluenced by the majority of members. "Gripe sessions" are occasionally held but they are always set firmly in the framework of the therapeutic ideology of Daytop. That is, they will entertain complaints about staff not living up to the ideals and standards of the community but will not seriously consider any grievances expressed against the paternalistic therapeutic ideology itself—"we know what is good for you and we will impose it on you as long as you stay here."

There are also regular grievance procedures whereby a resident can protest any action by a fellow member, including a person in authority over him. Most frequently used is the procedure for "dropping a slip" and taking a person to a group. Again, though, the framework of discussion is restricted by the group ideology. Ideally a relatively junior resident may get a more senior resident to "cop to a mistake" in the way he treated him, either voluntarily or under pressure from a group leader more senior than both of them, but in no case will one get any senior resident to agree that some basic rule of requirement is unnecessary or wrong. The Concept itself is not open to challenge.

In practice residents sometimes have found it difficult or even impossible to get a senior resident to cop to any mistakes in the application of the rules of the Concept. This is more liable to happen with coordinators or other residents of equivalent seniority, for they run groups themselves and have no one more senior in the group to put pressure on them. Ideally the resident with a complaint may appeal to the more senior person for justice but in practice this is an uncertain business.

In theory there are grievance procedures which should ensure justice but in practice there are many loopholes through which unfair staff and senior residents can escape. They can represent the complaint as being a symptom of "baby attitudes" or a desire to "punch holes in the Concept." They have to be careful that they are not noticed and confronted about it by someone on their own level or above, though. Nevertheless injustices inevitably occur in Daytop and the grievance procedures do not, of course, always work the way they are supposed to. The best grievance procedures in the world are not secure against unfair administrators. And it can be no surprise that some of the persons exercising authority in Daytop do so unfairly and defend themselves against legitimate grievances by unfair means. They are, after all, still in the course of their own treatment: they mostly have had little experience in exercising authority but plenty of experience as victims of unfair authority figures, and they are operating under a great deal of stress and anxiety.

We have noted that the Daytop power structure is monolithic and totalitarian, and that the Concept is not open to challenge. The actions and decisions of those individuals in authority are, however. In practice specific policies are not as open to challenge as they are supposed to be but there is nevertheless some occasional airing of grievances.

VARIANTS OF THE ENCOUNTER GROUP

We should note that a number of variations are played upon the basic theme of the encounter group as we have just described and analyzed it. We have already referred to the difference between encounter groups, properly so-called, and static groups. The latter have a fixed composition from week to week, while the former (encounter groups) change their composition according to the way the slips come out. Otherwise the dynamics or group processes are broadly similar in both. "Peer groups" are sometimes organized, bringing residents who entered Daytop at around the same time together in a group, sometimes replacing static groups or at other times in addition to them. "Specials" are emergency groups convened in order to deal with special problems, usually within a particular department. Sometimes the coordinator of the department will convene the group and run it or, if the problems include his poor leadership, the guru or one of the directors will do so.

When a "special" is being held there is usually an exceptional amount of hostility to be released first. That is one of the main reasons why the special is needed—because the morale and functioning of the whole department is seriously affected and it is becoming an untherapeutic experience for residents working in that department.

Coordinators have their own groups, usually led by a staff member of director level. These may be regarded as peer groups, though they meet regularly at least once a week. Directors of both houses and corporation directors have their own groups but less often. During the annual retreats, ethnically selective groups are held for Blacks, Jews, Italians, and Puerto Ricans to meet separately and discuss their feelings about being a member of that ethnic group. Women's groups are also held occasionally for women to relate to some of the problems they have as women, which they feel they cannot initially discuss in mixed groups with men.

Aside from these groups where the membership principles are varied, two other versions of the encounter group are used in Daytop. The "probe" is an all-night group that lasts from eight to twelve hours. It is designed to focus more on emotions and less on behavior than normal encounter groups do and to focus on a certain theme, such as fears, parents, or sexual hangups. Since the probe lasts longer, a more intense atmosphere of trust can develop and residents can gain much from sharing their feelings, important experiences, and hangups. The principle of using a long time span to break down defenses is taken even further in the "marathon" group, which can run for thirty or forty hours. One sleep-break of a few hours is allowed in the middle and snacks are available throughout. Marathons may be held only a couple of times a year and they are remembered vividly by many residents as a landmark in their Daytop careers.

In the marathon each person relates his life story as a means of trying to let the others in the group know who he is. Many members of the marathon group experience an emotional breakthrough with tears being shed as defenses drop and painful feelings are released.

There is much close identification with the speaker and tears are shed by everyone concerned. After the breakthrough the person who has related may reach out and ask for love from another member of the group. This is terribly hard for most people to do, and when he has taken the chance (of being refused) and the two embrace in the middle of the group, it is a very poignant moment for all.

Participating in a marathon generally makes a person start to see fellow participants in a new light. As one resident put it, "You see how beautiful other people are." A special bond develops between residents who have been through a marathon together and have been involved in an intimate way. Friendships often begin from this experience. Those who still refuse to trust or share throughout the whole marathon feel acutely isolated and those who give away just a little, knowing they are holding back a lot more, harbor guilt feelings that they may take to another group or perhaps to a trusted friend first. It is also possible that they may hold onto these guilt feelings and thus jeopardize their personal growth. It appears, however, that for the majority of those who participate in Daytop marathon groups, it is an occasion for peak experiences, having great importance for their emotional growth.

The encounter group, including the variants just mentioned, functions on two distinct levels: (1) as a therapeutic tool vital to the personal growth of the resident; and (2) as a safety valve for the release of feelings, especially the hostile feelings that are partly engendered by the high-pressure structure of the house itself. Once more we see the close interrelationship of social control and therapeutic process in the structure of this community.

6 / Therapeutic process and personal growth

It is conventional in presenting an analysis of a culture to make a distinction between the "native theory," or the ideas which the members of that culture employ to explain certain phenomena, and the imported theory developed by outsiders with a professional interest (including but not limited to the social scientist). In the case of Daytop this distinction is blurred for several reasons. One is that interested professionals have helped to formulate Daytop ideology, are currently involved in its activities to some extent, and are in communication with staff and residents. Dr. Daniel Casriel was Medical–Psychiatric Superintendent of Daytop at the time of this study and, as such, a part-time staff member. He has theorized about the psychodynamics of Daytop. In collaboration with David Deitch* he has experimented with Daytop techniques in his private psychiatric practice, evolved new approaches, refined the theories and the two of them have put their techniques into practice at Daytop. Another professional greatly interested in Daytop, who has spent time as a resident and theorized about the "Daytop dynamic" is O. Hobart Mowrer, Research Professor in Psychology at the University of Illinois. By means of occasional lectures and seminars conducted by Deitch, Casriel, and Mowrer, as well as by informal talks with senior and experienced staff, the professional perspective has to a significant extent percolated into the "native" culture of Daytop. However, this professional input remains a minor ingredient in a culture largely inherited from Synanon.

If there is no sharp or clear line between professional and native theories, though, there are distinct differences between residents as to how sophisticated an understanding they have of the social-psychological processes at work here. This is partly a matter of time and seniority, for it takes time to learn these apsects of the culture. Partly it is a matter of intelligence and aptitude for, or interest in, theoretical explanations. So even at the same levels of seniority, some residents have a greater understanding of the theory than others who have been in residence for the same length of time. In addition, too, there are matters of chance that have a short-term effect—for example, if a person is out of the house on a trip when one of the infrequent lectures is delivered. In the long run, though, such knowledge is reinforced and spread around the membership of the house as it is brought up in later seminars and data sessions, or repeated in the course of the normal routine.

* Deitch (1973) has recently published a paper on the Daytop therapeutic process.

DAYTOP THEORY IN THE COURSE OF DAILY ROUTINE

There are various occasions in the normal, routine life of Daytop when reference is likely to be made to aspects of this theory of resocialization. For example, before a haircut or other learning experience is given out, the COD briefs the other staff and residents who will assist him, and in these briefings there is usually an explanation of what the person has done to require the haircut or other learning experience. A full justification includes reference, at least by implication, to the theory underlying the decision. For example:

> We're giving him this to teach him that sneaking behind someone's back is dishonest. He's got to learn to be man enough to tell people to their face what he is bothered about. He goes around here acting so positive he must think he is well already. But he's still a stand-up dope-fiend and this should help him to start changing some of his dope-fiend attitudes.

In terms of social-psychological theory, two important points are being alluded to here. One is that the individual needs to change important attitudes which he has either deluded himself into thinking are already changed or which he does not know he still has. The second point, implied but not stated outright, is that direct confrontation is the best way to make a person change.

The COD's explanation is for the benefit of the group administering the learning experience, so that they can do the job with conviction and believe in the rightness of the decision. They may repeat the reasoning to the person actually receiving the sanction at that time. Sometimes it is important that a resident just be told "You have been doing ______. We don't tolerate that sort of behavior in here. So cut it out. Got that, stupid?" Such cases are covered by their own specific part of the theory. This asserts that in dealing with persons who are highly adept at making excuses for their behavior (which they often accept to be immoral and inexpedient), it is necessary to assault their self-confidence, based as it is on their ability to rationalize away unacceptable behavior. The assault says in effect, as those administering a haircut might actually say,

> Your thinking is too fucked up for us to reason with you. Your *thinking* is what got you here. For now, just do as we say. Trust that we know what is good for you better than you do. Although you don't like this, just consider the fact that the people who are telling you this have been where you are at now and we have got into something better, because we listened to someone who told us what we are telling you now.

The more sophisticated coordinators, the house director, and assistant director generally have the kind of understanding of the theory underlying the decisions they make to be able to explain everything we have just presented in our examples, though they might not do it quite so formally. The person who received the kind of haircut described is expected to go away from it and follow the orders he was given, whether he likes it or not—and usually, of course, he will not like it at all. Later he may ask to sit down with one of the senior members of the house, usually one of the people who gave him the haircut, to talk about his difficulties in understanding and accepting it. Then, certainly, the senior person will explain all the reasons, drawn from the social-psychological theory of Daytop, for the way they treated him. In the earlier and middle stages of a person's Daytop development, when stubbornness, the excessive use of rationalizations, and hiding behind "images" (more of this shortly) are major obstacles to growth, residents are expected to conform first and look for the reasons later. At later stages in a person's growth, he will be given the reasons for specific demands that are made on him. The reasons for this practice again take us back to the theory, which makes assumptions about the psychology of the typical addict and about the methods to which he is more or less likely to respond.

What we wish to illustrate here is the way theoretical explanations of the therapeutic process enter into the process itself and the degree to which theoretical explanations are utilized in different situations. This itself can be explained by reference to the social-psychological theory of Daytop. In order to make this point, we have used the single example of someone being given a haircut or other learning experience. There are, of course, numerous situations where aspects of Daytop theory are used, both to justify and explain an action and to teach the resident the Concept bit by bit. They include the following: during the first part of morning meeting when the COD is dealing with individual and collective delinquencies; in encounter groups when the person playing the role of "therapist" explains to the person in the "hot seat" why the group has treated him a certain way and why it is making certain demands on him; in lectures, seminars, and data sessions, where the purpose is simply to expound the theories underlying the Concept; in morning administrative meetings held by the house director for all coordinators, where they discuss how they are handling problems that are more than merely routine. Here both problems of individual residents and problems of work organization are discussed and the director offers criticism and suggestions. He refers to the same Daytop theory expounded at lower echelons, but in a manner befitting the stage of development and relative sophistication that these individuals have attained. Slowly but surely, an understanding of Daytop theory filters down from the top.

Every resident who has been in the house more than a few weeks has absorbed some elements of the Daytop theory and most can be found "running the data" to each other, that is, explaining to a peer who has not been doing what he should *why* it is important or explaining how he himself has to make a special effort in a certain direction.

THE THEORY: MAIN POSTULATES

Having examined the way in which theoretical explanations enter into daily interaction in the Daytop social system, we must now turn to review the main features of the theory itself. Its simplicity is an extremely important feature of the social-psychological theory of Daytop. It does not depend on an elaborate jargon of technical terms; nor does it postulate a complex model of psychological functioning or change. It is far simpler than psychoanalysis. Therefore it is not too hard for a group lacking formal education (most are high school drop-outs) to absorb, understand, and teach this theory—especially since it relates to their vital and all-consuming interest in changing themselves. Also, it is taught mainly in small, easily digested doses, nearly always in connection with a *concrete* example that they can readily understand. And so we move on to the main postulates of Daytop's psychological theory.

Images and the Need to Eradicate Them Addicts, and others with poor self-images, tend to cultivate "images" and hide behind them. Lacking good feelings about themselves *for* themselves, they seek good feelings about themselves for external characteristics. So they cultivate the dress, speech patterns, and other behavioral traits of (for example) the "tough guy" or the "super-cool" hipster, the hippie, the sex-star, or the intellectual. Behind this image cringes the fearful, inadequate-feeling person, trying to find happiness in the favorable responses of others to his image, his "act." Part of the image is that of addict or drug user.

From the time a person enters Daytop, starting with his interview, his image is stripped away from him. In the interview he is forced to answer questions as the real but frightened person behind the image, not as the "tough guy" or "cool guy" he wishes to present himself as. When the "prospect" has to agree (even though he may not really accept it deep down inside) that he is "stupid" and "a baby," his former image—no matter what it was—is shattered at least temporarily. If he stays at Daytop after the interview, all the external "props" he has used to maintain his image formerly are taken away from him: his long hair is cut short, his beard and mustache are shaved, his clothing and ornaments are removed and he is issued standard work clothes. He is also deprived of all his former social contacts, including fellow junkies, pushers, police, and parents, all of whom in their different ways may have helped to reinforce his unrealistic self-image—both the addict or drug user part of it and the other part (hippie, etc.). This is not to say that wearing long hair or exceptionally "sharp" clothes is necessarily indicative of a false "image." The attitude of the wearer is determinant. If he has a need for his hair or his sharp clothes to the point where he is acutely embarrassed to be seen in any other attire, then he probably has an image problem. There is no limit whatsoever to the possible range of external symbols with which a person may build his image.

Stripped of his image, the Daytop resident is forced to see himself as he really is. The "tough guy" is scared of certain things, and the "wise guy" is stupid in many ways. He is helped in this extremely painful process by his peers who confront him in encounter groups and practically around the clock about the way he acts and the way he feels about himself. Many residents say that this is the hardest thing of all about being a resident in Daytop, having to see yourself as you really are. What a person sees at this point is a lot of serious faults he must change and the prospect can be terrifying. This is one reason why so many split from Daytop.

For people to stay in spite of these unpleasant revelations there must be considerable pressure on them (for example, knowing that they will go to jail for a long time if they leave) or there must be enough emotional support within the house to help them weather the storms. Preferably there should be both. In fact it is possibly the most important feature of Daytop and a few similar programs that they provide at the same time merciless methods of making people face themselves and effective ways of "patching them up" and providing emotional support. This is provided by the constant availability of people willing to talk to a resident who is uptight; the vigilance of residents in watching for peers who may be uptight but not seeking help; the readiness of those who become aware of a fellow resident in distress to identify with him, telling about how they have felt (and perhaps still do feel) the same as he does, how they respect him for being open and honest enough to look at himself, how they have confidence in his ability to make the changes he wants to make, how good he will start to feel when he struggles to do "what he knows he has to," just as they themselves did.

This kind of moral and emotional support may be given in the setting of the encounter group or in the privacy of someone's office or room. The setting is immaterial; what is crucial is that this is a *personal* form of concern and help—that the person who is receiving help feels that the helper (or would-be helper) is personally concerned and can personally identify with the way he is feeling. This kind of relationship in which people can be "for real" with each other is what Daytop has to offer to the person whose image has been taken away. It is an integral part of the "treatment," the culture of the group, and it is the ultimate reward or goal that is held up to Daytop residents to justify the sacrifices they are asked to make. Beyond just living without dependence on drugs, Daytop offers the chance to learn to be "for real," to cultivate genuine, satisfying relationships with other people, free of phony images. Indeed, the only way to be sure that one can live without drugs, so Daytop teaches, is to develop the kind of inner strength based on the ability to form real relationships with other people and good feelings about oneself. In order to achieve these two things a person must give up his dependence on superficial, external images.

Dealing with Feelings The psychological model in use at Daytop starts out from the assertion that all people have certain primitive or "gut-level" feelings. The main ones are rage or *anger* when we are thwarted or prevented (intentionally or otherwise) from getting something we want, *hurt* when rebuffed or ignored by someone from whom we seek a favorable response, *fear,* and *loneliness.* These feelings are believed to be found across all different cultures. They are sometimes referred to in Daytop as "the monster in your belly." People may be classified into different character types according to how they deal with these primitive feelings. One type of person simply gives vent to these feelings when they arise, even though such behavior is most often socially taboo. They vent their anger by yelling at or hitting whatever or whoever gets in their way; they sulk when their feelings are hurt, and so forth. This type "acts off his belly" in Daytop parlance; he is uncontrolled and unsocialized. The second type is highly socialized or, from the standpoint of this theory, *over*-socialized. These people repress the gut feelings and deny their existence. They swallow their hurt and anger. They say "I don't really mind." For them the head, not the belly, runs their lives. The third type of person is aware of his gut-level feelings, but recognizes that there are sanctions against certain spontaneous expressions—especially anger, so he curbs his behavior. His head controls his belly but he is still in touch with the latter. He does not displace his feelings onto other objects (for example, by scapegoating or "coming out sideways") as the repressed person is prone to do. This third type expresses his feelings selectively. Unlike the over-socialized or repressed character type, he is in touch with his feelings; unlike the first type, he can control his impulses and refrain from venting his feelings in ways that will be costly to him.

Drug addicts may belong to either type one or type two. What Daytop attempts to do is transform them into type three. In encounter groups anyone who claims that he never feels angry is ridiculed and teased until *that* makes him angry, for it is maintained that everyone should express anger in groups by yelling and cursing in the accepted Daytop way. At all times in Daytop self-control is required. Even in groups a person must wait his turn and keep his seat. At other times people must learn to keep the lid on their feelings, especially those of anger and hurt, and express them at the right place and time. The Daytop structure is thus equipped to help both types one and two with their characteristic problems in this area.

As one resident in reentry stage was heard to say, he still gets scared but has learned to handle those feelings. Previously he would go to dope when he felt scared. In some ways he now has *more intense* feelings than he used to. For example, when he sees a movie, he has a greater emotional reaction now than he used to. Thus from Daytop he has learned to deal with his feelings differently and to have more control over his behavior; he has also learned greater depth of feeling. He has grown on both levels.

The double-edged rule is summarized as "hold and dump." Hold your angry feelings until group, then dump all the "garbage." Also talk about your other feelings, both good and bad, to other residents to whom you feel close. Confront other people with your feelings about them personally. If you have guilt feelings on account of something you have done, spill it out in front of your fellows. Then you can "clean it up" in an appropriate way (perhaps by taking a learning experience), be rid of the guilt feelings, and continue to grow.

By holding onto garbage a person increases the likelihood of reacting impulsively. One can hold only so much before exploding. The more you hold, the more likely it is that the next strain that arouses bad feelings will tip you over the edge and lead to some disastrous reaction or lead you to split. Where guilt is concerned a similar thing occurs. To get rid of it you have to cop to what you did. If it is discovered and someone asks "who did this?," your guilt feelings will kick up inside you. If you fail to cop to it, then guilt will assail you at every reminder of the event until you break down and either cop to it finally or leave. The inevitable strains of living in this environment, on top of the guilt, will ensure that the breaking point is soon reached.

It is possible that drug addicts are characteristically "touchy" and get enraged or get their feelings hurt easily. What is more to the point, though, is that they are manifestly unable to handle their feelings when aroused; hence the insistence on not "reacting" and the provision of legitimate dumping places (primarily the encounter group but sometimes in one-to-one talks with staff). In the short term the dumping grounds provide the opportunity for people to restructure their feelings—to learn to trust other people more and to have more self-esteem—as well as to learn new coping mechanisms; notably to confront others in a restrained way when something in their relationship bothers them, instead of leaving resentments unstated and misunderstandings unclarified to fester with time and build up unbearable levels of bad feeling.

Residents generally get the message that in Daytop they must control their tendency to "react" and must act as if they were positive in attitude. Sometimes, though, they fail to get the equally important message that while they must do these things, they must also talk about their negative feelings at the appropriate times and places. (They should not normally talk to newer residents about this but should go to older residents or to their peers.) This important mistake is known as "playing it safe" or acting "ultrapositive." Among the most senior residents and staff it is acknowledged that the resident who *never* acts out by violating a rule is more of a problem to them (from a therapeutic point of view) than the one who occasionally acts out and has to be disciplined or "shot down." By acting out the resident gives clues to the nature of his problem and gives his would-be helpers some idea of "where he is at" and what kind of help he needs. By getting himself into trouble and taking the consequences, he forces himself to face his problems and the behavior that needs changing. Otherwise it is all too easy for the resident whose "act as if" is too complete to fool himself into thinking that he is much further along than he really is. He may believe that he can cope on the outside without all the group support and the external controls that keep him going in Daytop. In that frame of mind, he is very prone to split at his first serious difficulty and come to grief. In this sense, then, *some* acting out is necessary for the Daytop therapeutic process to work.

One institution that encourages residents to relate to their negative feelings without fear of being punished for them is the so-called "negative session." This is a bull session in which residents reminisce about the crazy, negative things they used to do or dream about doing when they were on the street and which they still sometimes yearn for. Negative sessions usually take place at night and are always conducted by a staff member above coordinator status. Most often these are all-male affairs. Women have an opportunity to do the same at certain times (for example, during the occasional women's retreats) but it seems that women engage in this practice less often than men.

A second function is served by the negative session, apart from the important therapeutic one of keeping residents in touch with their negativity so that they should be able to deal with it instead of just trying to repress it. This other function is to help residents to identify with staff more readily, once they see them as having shared the same negative past and, in a sense, sharing the same negative desires still—though they have learned not to indulge them. Out of the negative session comes an enhanced feeling of camaraderie among all the participants.

The negative session serves as an officially sanctioned substitute for the informal talk about former exploits that took place on the streets. The important difference is that an experienced staff member is in charge of the session and can keep it within a positive frame of reference—though not obtrusively so. In one sense, though, the negative session violates Daytop values, for it permits residents to boast of previous negative exploits and to receive some esteem on the basis of them. If the person who tops everyone else's exploits in the telling is the staff member who is running the negative session, this is strictly speaking a compromise of Daytop values, insofar as he is encouraging other residents to admire him for his negative exploits rather than for his present positive achievements. In practical terms, though, it may well be that this is the only way to get certain kinds of residents to start to respect staff. Note that the negative session is only an occasional event and that the great majority of the time staff appear before residents in their "positive" capacity.

Fight, Flight, and Withdrawal Another aspect of character differences that is important for understanding the addict and how to help him change concerns his typical, spontaneous response to situations in which he feels endangered. One type of person typically responds with the feeling of *rage* and the act of *fighting.* A second type responds with the feeling of *fear* and the act of *fleeing* from that situation. This is the traditional "fight or flight" distinction. To this Casriel has added a third category which, he believes, defines the typical response of the character disordered person, including the drug addict. This is the defense mechanism of emotional detachment or *withdrawal.*

This aspect of Daytop psychological theory is the only one we shall cover here which is relatively esoteric, and not widely understood among Daytop staff, let alone residents, in the abstract, theoretical terms in which Casriel propounds it. We outline it here, not only for its intrinsic interest, but because several of the lower-level theories that are current among residents are (theoretically) dependent on it. In effect, we are now leaving aside our account of "native theories" of the Daytop therapeutic process to interject a technical note from the professional observer.

Casriel explained his theory in a paper presented to the Annual Meeting of the American Psychiatric Association in 1966, thus:

> By successfully removing themselves from the pain of reacting to stress, they [people who use the defense mechanism of detachment or withdrawal] have detached themselves and spend their energy reinforcing, by encapsulating, their isolation to a non-painful state of functioning. Like its sister defense mechanism of fight and flight, the psychodynamic defense of detachment may have been a very realistic one in the individual's early experience. Once patterned and ingrained, detachment very frequently becomes an intrapsychic fortress of one's own making. The patient has taken flight without fear into a fortress in which he feels secure, but realistically in which he is quite isolated, incapacitated, and imprisoned. His original fortress has become his stockade. The longer the individual stays in his own jail, the thicker the walls become by secondary encapsulation, with the result that the individual is less and less able to cope with the problems of everyday living.
>
> Once this intrapsychic world with relatively little tension is evolved, the individual will overtly or covertly fight anyone who attempts to remove him from his prison-fortress . . . from his encapsulated shell of detachment. Once the adaptational mechanism of withdrawal and detachment is evolved and becomes a primary mechanism, the standard psychoanalytic techniques using introspection and observation are useless. The individual patient, though he hears, cannot be reached . . . though he knows, he will not change. He will avoid the truth with or without outright lies. Though he may pay lip service to treatment, he spends conscious and/or unconscious psychic energy in reinforcing his defensive detachment by a secondary encapsulation. A pastime which has in addition a pleasurable

component—the encapsulative shell can be made out of alcohol, drugs, narcotics, homosexuality, delinquency, or just a quiet emotional detachment from all meaningful emotional relationships without necessarily being asocial or anti-social. As a matter of fact, encapsulation could be socially productive—the shell can be reading in the library every spare minute, up in the attic with a stamp collection, down in the cellar with the tool chest, out at the links with the golf clubs, or in the office with patients. The detached person identifies with others with the same shells, which gives him pleasurable reassurance and reinforcement. . .

The problem in treatment becomes obvious. To effectuate treatment, one must first remove the encapsulating shell and prevent the individual from withdrawing into detachment by acquiring or running into any other kind of encapsulating shell. Then, once exposed to the light of reality, powerless to isolate himself without his fortress-prison-stockade of an encapsulated shell, he is in a position to be taught how to grow up.

Encapsulation Most residents are familiar with the concept of "encapsulation" which corresponds precisely to Casriel's concept of withdrawal. Although the theory of three modes of response to danger is barely known in Daytop, the dangers of encapsulation are constantly emphasized. In daily life in the house encapsulation shows itself in repeated acts of forgetfulness—forgetting to check in or out when entering or leaving the building, forgetting to turn lights off, forgetting to clean one's room or complete some assigned task, forgetting to collect one's laundry, and in many other instances. Because repeated forgetfulness is considered, officially and explicitly, to be a sign of encapsulation, a very stern view is taken of it. Without an understanding of this connection plus the critical role played by encapsulation in the personality structure of the addict, many of the learning experiences that residents receive would indeed seem harsh and undeserved. For example, a resident is made to apologize to the whole house for his "stupidity"; others have been made to wear large signs referring to the encapsulation. Such responses to forgetfulness become understandable, when it is appreciated that forgetfulness is a common symptom of encapsulation and that encapsulation is one of the prime characteristics of the addict. It supports other aspects of the typical addict personality structure; for example, his inability to take account of the adverse consequences of present behavior or to control impulses.

"Be aware," residents are constantly being told in Daytop and "don't be encapsulated." We have discussed forgetfulness and the response to this in Daytop; we must also consider another aspect of the encapsulation problem: the drug addict is generally a very asocial person who has little communication with other people except for limited relationships of expediency for the sharing of drugs and "works" (hypodermic needle and boiling apparatus for dissolving the powder in water). If his relationships go beyond this, they are mediated through some "image," as discussed in an earlier section of this chapter. The fact that he usually has no meaningful human relationships contributes greatly to the low self-esteem of the addict and his fearfulness in dealing with people. It encourages him to cling more tightly to the subjective security of his encapsulation—through drugs, through his image, and sometimes through some obsessive interest in which he invests all his energies. It keeps him within his shell or capsule, away from meaningful exchanges with other people—narcissistic, self-pitying, rationalizing his weaknesses instead of changing them.

Residents relax and talk during free time. Although the young man wearing the cardboard sign has recently "messed up," he is not shunned as an outcast but is treated as a human being and encouraged to talk about his difficulties. His sign reads, "My belly is full of fear. I must trust or it will destroy me. Help!"

In Daytop residents are not allowed to isolate themselves or spend time alone; they are required to "relate," to communicate with others. This policy is supposed to help residents pry themselves out of their shells, and keep them from wallowing in self-pity, from feeding themselves excuses for rejecting the unpleasant truths that confront them here. To a significant extent it appears to work.

Residents who have a keen interest in an area such as music, for example, will be forbidden to practice or even talk about it for a while. It is too easy for them to relate to other people through this single interest and avoid looking at themselves in terms of their responsibilities as people—as husband, father, son, friend, and so forth. It is too easy for them to get good feelings from their expertise in one area and to ignore the bad feelings that should be motivating them to change their irresponsible behavior. Just as efforts are made to strip away a person's image when he enters Daytop, similar efforts are made to remove any other "crutches" he may have been using to support his crippled personality. Without his crutches, it is believed, he will be more likely to do something about the problems that have been crippling him.

"The kind of people we are," both new residents and visitors are told by more experienced Daytop residents, "we don't learn from people being nice to us." This, it is explained, is why pull-ups must be made in such a fashion as to thoroughly embarrass the person being pulled up; this is why people who "goof up" have to be "dumped" ("Don't do that, stupid"); this is why haircuts and learning experiences are used. This is why the Daytop resident finds that his mistakes are exaggerated and overdramatized in order to get through his encapsulation and make him understand, in spite of his automatic rationalizations and excuses, that he must change his behavior. This is why taking something without first getting permission is labelled unequivocally as "stealing" and giving an explanation that is incomplete or misleading is defined as "lying." Again, for example, leaving a screwdriver out in the parking lot may seem a trivial error, but as a symptom of a state of encapsulation that has protected an addict from seeing the reality and consequences of his life style, it is far more serious. It would, presumably, be possible to investigate the psychodynamic origins of his encapsulation but the Daytop approach is different: it is to blast through the door of the safe, rather than to spend a very long time trying to disassemble the locks and hope that someone can then make a new key.

This is what Daytop people mean when they talk of junkies being "killed with kindness," meaning that the efforts of traditionally trained counselors, social workers, and others who only know how to point things out gently, without hurting their feelings too much, fail to induce any changes in their junkie clients and hence "kill" them or fail to prevent them from killing themselves. What is needed, Daytop staff members maintain, is to confront the junkie with the stark reality of what he is doing in terms that he can understand, in unmistakable black and white.

Daytop staff have long known which methods of teaching were relatively successful and which were unsuccessful with "people like us," either as a matter of simple empirical experience or as a piece of traditional folklore brought from Synanon and confirmed by their continuing experience. Casriel's theory relates these methods to the encapsulation process, buttressed by the addict's extreme facility at rationalizing and excusing his weaknesses. His theory relates two crucial ideas: the role of encapsulation and the need for forceful methods of teaching, so that each throws new light on the other and both gain additional significance from their place within the larger theory. All this is generally unknown to Daytop residents, though they do make extensive use of the two specific propositions (encapsulation and forceful teaching) separately.

PHASES OF PERSONAL GROWTH

Senior Daytop staff can describe the typical Daytop career as involving certain distinct phases, punctuated by "humps" or critical junctures at which certain difficulties, which have been latent during the preceding phase, surface and create a new crisis for the resident. Commonly the crisis takes the form of his wanting to split or "go into a bag" (depression). It would be a mistake to generalize too much about the course of development of Daytop residents. Some do not experience definite humps or critical junctures at all; and, obviously, they vary in frequency and intensity among those who do encounter them.

Two informants who have been quoted earlier, Felix Donawa and Richie Rode, were asked about how they perceived changes in themselves while they were residents of Daytop. Both said that changes seemed gradual and almost imperceptible. Usually they only become aware of them in retrospect. This is an important point to keep in mind in respect to the "humps" theory, which makes it seem as if the resident is aware of what he is experiencing at the time and aware of its significance. But this is not necessarily so.

In response to a question about how his attitude to the house changed, Felix gave the following answer. Note that he considers the social expectations in the house not only responsible for *causing* the change in his attitude but also for signaling to him the fact that he had begun to change.

> I think when it really started changing I might have been around like 9 months. And I think what made it change was the fact that . . . people started expecting certain things of me, people started looking at me to assume some kind of postures, to be a certain type of role model and so forth . . . like they're saying you've been around here 9 months and there's a certain amount of responsibility you should have attained. Certain people recognize this and the people who was just coming in and was below me was looking kinda up to me in certain degrees—I think this is what sorta began to tell me or where I began to realize that I must have changed. 'Cos I couldn't see any physical change. And for the most part I knew that in certain instances I was somewhat negative, thinking-wise, and every once in a while I would act out in a way. But I think that the fact that you was getting the demand from above and below, you know, and the responsibility that you was expected to assume and the responsibility that you *was* actually doing—I think this was when I first realized that I was changing."

Richie Rode was asked whether he accepted the idea of turning points in a person's development in Daytop but he did not really accept this way of describing the process:

A: I see it more as . . . you're going through a therapeutic community and each day you're experiencing something. Gradually, you don't realize it, but you're starting to change. Usually you can't see the change because all of those little things are happening, one on top of the other. You're still feeling the same, or in some cases you're even feeling worse. You have a lot of downs when you're going through this kind of a process. I think you realize that you're starting to change when you've been around maybe six months and you start to realize that you're doing something that you never did before in your life. And then you try to figure out "why am I doing these things"? You're accepting things for the first time in your life. And you say "Gee whiz, I'm starting to change."

Q: Can you relate that to yourself?

A: Well, I guess the best example for me would be that the thing I always wanted to do was to run out and get high. After about six months I hadn't gotten high and I was learning to relate to those feelings of wanting to do something but yet not doing it. And doing a lot of things that I never did before—like being responsible, getting up in the morning, doing my job,

> doing it properly, sticking to it until it was done, facing a lot of things. And I started to realize that I was changing because I was doing all of these things without getting high.

With all these cautions about oversimplifying our models of personal growth in Daytop, we return to the theory of humps propounded by some senior staff in Daytop. This account can be taken on two different levels: as a set of beliefs held by staff and used by them to interpret fluctuations in the developmental careers of Daytop residents, beliefs that may or may not be closely related to fact, or as a theory that can be *assumed* to correspond in some significant measure to reality and hence can serve as an important guide to the nature of that reality. We can, I believe, make use of it on both levels, by assuming that it is fairly accurate for a significant proportion of successful residents.

The humps which commonly arise in a resident's Daytop career were described for my benefit and at my request by one of the two co-directors in 1968, Charles Devlin. I was prompted to ask about this by having heard talk among residents of the "six months hump" and other "humps" (common times of special difficulty in one's Daytop career). So far as I can tell, residents would not normally hear a complete account of the three humps as I did, but would normally meet these concepts through the counseling of senior residents or staff when they ran into one of these periods of difficulty in their own development or when they heard a fellow resident who had already run into one talk about it. Residents in this situation would be reassured that the difficulties they were experiencing are common for someone at their stage in their Daytop development. They would be helped to understand why and how these difficulties arise and what to do to overcome them and move on successfully to the next stage of their development. The following account is an elaboration of the beliefs of senior Daytop personnel in terms of this investigator's understanding of Daytop theory and practice.

The first hump is the "three-month hump" which follows the period of settling into the new routine, referred to as "the honeymoon," though this label is misleading insofar as it tends to gloss over the difficulty many residents have in learning not to react and not to be forgetful. The point which is validly emphasized by the term "honeymoon" is that this initial period in the house, for all its hardships, is nothing serious compared to the difficulties yet to come. The first time these difficulties become apparent is around three months. At about this time (though it may come a lot sooner or later for some individuals) the resident begins to realize that "he is not just playing games." In other words, he begins to realize that he has become involved in something that entails a great degree of commitment and that has profound implications for the course of his life.

Initially, it is very likely that he entered Daytop with very tainted motivation—to save himself from going to jail (after the judge had given him the option of Daytop with a suspended sentence or serving that sentence right away), to get his family "off his back," to escape from the pressures of life "on the street" and the daily hassles for survival. His motivation to get into Daytop may have been strong but it was probably not very pure—in the sense of involving a determination to change himself. This is generally true, despite the fact that the interview procedure, makes an impression on new residents. Usually, this impression is not strong enough to make him decide immediately to accept the whole ideological package that Daytop offers. The implications of such acceptance are too vast, his grasp of what he is getting into is still very limited at that point, and his junkie defenses are still operating—though uncommonly large holes have been knocked in them. Over the period of his first months in Daytop, though, as the day-to-day worries subside, an awareness of the larger reality of what he has gotten himself into dawns on him and scares him. This is the so-called "three-month hump."

He realizes—often hazily—that what is expected of him goes far beyond the various expectations for specific behavior. He is expected to strive to be honest and open, to trust people, to learn to make real friendships, and to invest something of himself in really meaningful relationships for the first time. He is expected to put aside the shell in which he has previously encapsulated himself and permit himself to be open and vulnerable to other people. At this point he has little faith in his ability to do this and, even more importantly, very little conviction that it is worth it to him to take these enormous risks. He does not know, but he doubts, whether he dare step into this terrifying, unknown territory, fear of which (felt unconsciously perhaps) may well have been what started him on the path of encapsulation and addiction in the first place.

Stated this way it is a miracle that any resident stays on past his three-month hump. Many do not, of course. That *any* stay is due to the efficacy of senior residents in reassuring those going through this hump with many references to their own similar experiences. It is also perhaps due to the fact that three-month residents do not generally perceive their situation in such clear or dramatic terms as those in which we have depicted it here.

The six-month hump is in part, a reappearance of the same fears that surfaced in the three-month hump and partly a new problem. The new problem is a struggle between the resident's emergent desires to "jump on board" and identify himself with his role models in Daytop and the positive values for which they stand, and recurring nostalgia for certain aspects of his former life. He wants to become responsible, honest, and caring like his Daytop role models, but at the same time he still yearns for the kind of negative and irresponsible "good times" he used to have, for the luxury of just not bothering about anything and not having to struggle the way he must in Daytop. He experiences this conflict between the positive and the negative desires within him and questions the worth of the herculean efforts he has made up to this point. At the same time he experiences again the same fears of his three-month hump, fears at how appallingly big an undertaking he has become involved in.

Around one year in Daytop comes another hump. This time the problem is the resident's overconfidence. He thinks "now I'm well" and forgets that his newly developing strength and positive values have only been tested in the very special and protective environment to which he has so far been restricted. He chafes at the restrictions still placed on him, feeling that they are no longer necessary. Frequently, however, the one-year hump comes to a particular crisis when the resident is exposed to some situation, especially one outside the house, that is relatively unfamiliar to him and not structured along the lines of typical Daytop situations. In this situation he is confused and does not act as he should. He realizes this and, on his return to the house, tells a senior resident, as he is supposed to. The balloon of his overconfidence is cruelly burst and from the one extreme attitude of assuming "I'm well" he swings to the opposite extreme and concludes, "I haven't learned anything, I haven't really got anything down." This conclusion is just as false as the first one, for the truth lies somewhere in between. The problem for the senior residents who counsel others through their one-year hump is to get them to see this, as always with many references to their own experiences at this stage.

Another aspect of the one-year hump is that the Daytop resident at this stage comes to realize, as a result of the same kind of incident that we have already mentioned, that he has not given up as much of his old image as he believed. He may come to this realization on his own or it may be pointed out to him. Either way he sees that he has to give up more of his image that he has been holding onto in relatively subtle ways. He is afraid of doing so for all the same reasons indicated before in our analysis of the three-month hump including a fear of making himself vulnerable to other people, of committing himself to new, positive values that will always (seemingly) keep him struggling to live up to them without rest or relief.

At this point, as at other humps or crises, there is a strong tendency for him to think of splitting—running from the situation that arouses these painful fears. The role of the counselor, the senior resident, or staff member to whom this individual turns, is to help him look at the reality of the choices open to him. On the one hand, he can split from Daytop and return before long to his former way of life. Anyone who has split from Daytop has absorbed something from his stay, and his return to the old way of life is not at all the same as it once was. Such, at any rate, is the testimony of those who have returned to the house and been readmitted. The hassles are just as bad but the pleasures are gone. He has become too aware of what he is doing to enjoy things as before: drugs no longer give the same satisfaction, nor does he enjoy the company of former associates now that he has learned something about trust and honesty in human relationships. At the same time he is still bound to get rearrested soon and either go straight to jail to serve a suspended sentence already imposed on him or to be newly sentenced. With his record he stands likely to get a stiffer sentence than anything he has previously had.

Such is the reality of one option the resident who is ready to give up his struggle can make. The other choice is to stay and continue the struggle, believing that he can manage to get over the hurdles, clearing them one at a time, as others have done and are doing before his eyes. He will probably be told to reflect upon the good feelings about himself that he gained from earlier struggles and accomplishments and on the growing respect that he has been earning from his peers and seniors (including the very people he holds as his role models). By staying on and grappling with his difficulties like a man (or woman), he can look forward to a continuation of these rewards. By splitting he will be letting these people down, as well as himself. At these "humps" or critical junctures in a person's development, he faces with special poignancy the choice of carrying on or quitting.

It is certainly appreciated by Daytop staff that defining humps on the basis of particular time intervals is a gross approximation to reality, which is very variable as to timing and also as to the actual process whereby problems unfold in the case of different individuals.

We have outlined the theory of developmental stages in Daytop growth, a theory held among upper echelon staff and diffused bit by bit among other residents, generally the more senior ones. This is one aspect of Daytop social-psychological theory which is used almost exclusively among staff and no effort is made to teach it to other residents.

To conclude this chapter on personal growth, we can illustrate the kind of character structure that Daytop staff aim to create in residents, and which residents are supposed to be aiming to create in themselves, as they enter the final stages of the treatment process. In this quote, Richie Rode is describing the temptation to split and how one can deal with it rationally. In the early phases of treatment the resident needs someone else to persuade him to think rationally about his feelings of wanting to split, but, as he becomes more mature and internalizes Daytop norms of not acting "off your belly," he can contemplate the consequences of his choices by himself.

> There were times when I became an older resident when I'd be in New York or something and I had all of these restrictions on me—like I had to be back by 1 o'clock in the morning. I had to ride the train to the ferry, then the ferry and then the bus. A lot of times I wished I could just stay in New York and didn't have to go back. But at that time I knew it would only be a matter of time before I could do that. As you go on you learn to rationalize more and more why you shouldn't act off those feelings. You have the experience of being in the program and dealing with certain things. See, the biggest problem a drug addict has is that all of his past experiences have to do with him usually acting off whatever he feels and doing whatever he wants to do. So, when the feeling comes up the only thing that he has to relate back to, in terms of dealing with it, is to act off it or to run away. When a person has enough experiences where he has dealt with things in his past, that becomes a pattern of behavior for him to follow. As the pattern becomes bigger and deeper, he learns to rationalize more. In the beginning it's tough because he just has no answers for himself. He just has to go by what other people tell him. That's why it's important for the new kid to be pulled in properly.

7/Some basic requirements of a therapeutic community

BOUNDARIES

As a total institution Daytop has a rigid boundary separating it from the outside society, a boundary that imposes many restrictions on the behavior of residents and stringent requirements for acceptance as a resident. The procedures for processing applicants emphasize to them that acceptance into the group is a privilege only granted upon the prospect's agreement to conform and to accept the Daytop definition of the situation. Sometimes non-conforming members are thrown out; more often they choose to leave rather than to accept the consequences which fall to those who violate the basic rules of the house.

The most striking symbol of the boundary perhaps is the prospect chair. This is where the prospect seeking admission is required to sit. This is where the resident who plans to split is expected to sit and think over his decision before talking one more time with a staff member and older residents. This is where a resident is placed when he is felt by staff to be severely lacking in motivation and under consideration to be thrown out. A person sitting on the chair is poised at the boundary between Daytop and the outside society, either on his way in or on his way out.

Within the boundary, as a member of the Daytop group, the resident is subject to all the rules and restrictions of the house. Thus when he feels like doing something that is not permitted by the rules of the house, though it may be permitted outside, he becomes at that moment especially aware of the boundary. It is reflected in his not being allowed to come and go at will, to have communication with people outside Daytop without permission, to drink alcohol, to wear the clothes he wants, and so forth. The Daytop boundary not only restricts residents' access to activities and persons outside of Daytop, it simultaneously restricts the access of outsiders to residents. Thus relatives and friends must wait until the resident earns the right to communicate. In addition, they must be screened to ensure that they are not drug users.

Those who have split are much more rigidly and totally barred from access to Daytop and its residents. The most impenetrable barrier separates them from their erstwhile comrades. They are seen as having betrayed the group and those who tried to help them, and as having threatened the motivation of others by leaving. Because their presence would be a real and continuing threat, they are not allowed to visit the house—unless they are formally seeking reacceptance by sitting on the chair. Then they are usually subjected to a general meeting of the whole house. Those who have split are more or less shunned. Neither graduates nor residents who are allowed to go outside Daytop are permitted to socialize with them.

The Daytop boundary is obviously more penetrable to the senior resident who has earned various privileges permitting him contact with the outside than it is to the new resident who is purposely isolated. Indeed, the process of advancing in Daytop includes as an important component the widening of the resident's contacts with people outside of Daytop. This is formalized eventually (after about eighteen months) in the "reentry process" which contains broad guidelines for getting him progressively more involved, both functionally and socially, with the outside world. He will be given a job in the SPAN center or possibly (but not so often) allowed to take a regular job while continuing to live in the house. If he has not started to develop a social life outside of Daytop he will be confronted about this and reminded that he should make efforts in that direction. When the senior Daytop resident begins dating outside the house, he or she is expected to bring the partner to the house to meet some of the staff and be informally screened, rather along the lines of the Victorian family.

There are other ways in which the official barriers to the outside world are gradually eliminated in the course of a person's progress through Daytop. Once he is considered fairly responsible, he will be assigned to go on outside speaking engagements in the company of an older resident. Later, he may be assigned to work in the community relations department contacting outside business people to request donations and, when successful, picking them up. This work entails a high level of contact with the outside world and, partly for that reason, enjoys high prestige in the house. This work is gratifying (dealing with company executives as the representative of "Daytop Village, Incorporated") and, at the same time, exposes one to a lot of disappointment and rejection, which makes it a valuable growth experience.

"Confirmation" or graduation comes when a panel of directors has interviewed the resident and judged him mature enough to stand on his own feet, no longer needing the supervision of the house. Graduates may still stay with the Daytop organization if they wish, and may be offered a salaried post. However, they are completely free to work and live wherever they please.

Graduates are advised to remain in contact with Daytop, even if they choose to work and live elsewhere. This is partly on the sentimental grounds that "Daytop is your family." But there are also sound practical reasons for it. Strains will inevitably arise and their newly accustomed ways of coping with situations of strain will not be available on the outside. He will have no encounter groups and, more importantly, his attempts to confront others and discuss problems openly will sometimes be rebuffed. By periodic visits to Daytop, he can regain his psychic balance and "recharge his batteries."

The graduate going to live and work outside Daytop still remains, in a sense, within its boundaries—not physically now but as a member of a normative reference group or an ethical movement to which he gives allegiance. The whole point of the Daytop experience is to instill certain values, attitudes, and ways of coping.

To the extent that the Daytop graduate remains faithful to these, either as completely internalized ego ideals or superego demands, or as the expectations of his significant others, to that extent he is enclosed within the Daytop boundary and limits are placed on his behavior.

One of the controversial issues regarding the Daytop of 1967–1968 concerns the extent to which Deitch and his staff encouraged residents, especially as they approached confirmation, to consider continued membership affiliation with Daytop (or at least with another Concept program) as the only acceptable career. Apparently such pressure did develop in 1968, perhaps partly because most graduates were not vocationally qualified in any other area and attractive careers were opening up for the first time for Concept graduates as staff members in other drug programs. Also ideological pressures were indirectly influencing residents.

The graduate who chooses to stay in Daytop as a staff member has a more *concrete* boundary defining his lifespace than the graduate who leaves. In addition to the ethical constraints that both feel, the graduate who stays is subjecting himself to the continued evaluations of senior staff, which will determine his rate of career advancement. Also, he is continuing to live daily in the sight of the same people who have monitored his conduct for the last two years or so and therefore has a great deal more social support for continuing his new life style.

More than half of the early graduates did, in fact, stay with Daytop. This is a frequent point of criticism, it being implied that graduates could not manage to live independently. This is possibly true of some but not necessarily of all; as we have indicated the very compelling career reasons for a graduate to stay in this line of work. But the point remains that these graduates have not *proved* (to others or to themselves) that they can cope with more conventional jobs and with living independently. However, since 1969, significantly more graduates have taken work that is not in the field of drug rehabilitation. It is generally conceded that even those graduates who stay in the Concept are doing valuable work and are infinitely better citizens now than they were before entering Daytop. In addition, Daytop staff insist that it is natural for graduates to be more attracted to life in the Concept than in the outside world because of the love and honesty that they have come to value, which is found abundantly in Daytop and more rarely outside.

IDEOLOGY

There is a clear set of ideological beliefs expounded by the senior members that the newer members are required to accept. It is affirmed that addicts can change their way of life (and the presence of the older residents seems to prove it) but only if there is a great deal of mutual help. The help which one gives to a fellow member, it is held, benefits not only the recipient but also the donor. Even the newest novice is capable of giving some significant help to a fellow member: by showing him concern and reminding him when he violates one of the rules of the community.

In Daytop the addict is required and helped to redefine himself and his situation drastically. He is told to think of himself no longer as a drug-using adult but as an emotionally immature baby who has to learn from the beginning how to live as an adult. From his more advanced peers he hears "Like you, I was a baby but now I'm learning to be a man." With the aid of such role models, a resident begins to redefine himself or he leaves, for the restrictions in Daytop are quite intolerable if one does not accept the justification for them.

The psychological theory of Daytop holds that the addict uses drugs to withdraw from responsible involvement in life. Hence the problem is not so much one of addiction but rather of the personality problems that lead to withdrawal and drug dependence. Conventional treatment of the addict, either punishing him for his addiction or pitying and babying him for it, have no therapeutic value. On the contrary, they both tend to reinforce the addict in his behavior. What he gets at Daytop is "reality therapy," that is, unambiguous feedback on his behavior with insistent demands that he change it.

The newcomer sees that Daytop is an ongoing community. Older residents have a strong sense of loyalty to the Daytop community, realizing that through it they have begun to find a happier life. These residents stand as positive role models for newcomers; they demonstrate that addicts can change their way of life. They will encourage and pressure the newcomers to conform to the group, because it is their lifeboat and they do not want the newcomers on board to sink it. For these residents it is a source of pride and strength to know that they serve as models for the novices.

As a therapeutic community, perhaps the most significant characteristic of Daytop is that the sharp dichotomy between staff and inmate norms—typically found in prisons, mental hospitals, and schools—is not present here. Through its policy of selection and rigorous social control it keeps those residents who are not prepared to conform away from positions of influence in the group and constantly pressures them to change.

Membership in Daytop, unlike attendance at most conventional treatment programs, is a privilege and not a penalty. Membership offers definite gratifications in the form of warm comradeship, a growing pride in self, and hope for one's future prospects. It also entails hardships: the high level of conformity demanded to so many rules, the humiliating redefinition of self, and the relentless demands for honesty and efforts to change. The motivation that keeps a person there must, therefore, be strong. In the early days of Daytop most residents had heavy suspended jail sentences hanging over them but by 1968 only about half were in this position or on probation. Others are here because of pressure from families or friends, or from weariness with their way of life and fear of the risks of continuing it. There is a substantial split rate (over 50% of all those admitted split in the first eighteen months) but it would be even higher if Daytop staff could not confront residents with the reality of "what is there out there for you?" Many, evidently, ignore this and leave anyway but it seems to help some residents hang on and weather the rough times.

An interesting summary of Daytop ideology is provided by a document, displayed on a bulletin board in 1967, curiously entitled "The Unwritten (sic) Philosophy of Daytop." It lists the following ten principles, most of them covered in our earlier account of the Daytop Concept.

1. Honesty
2. Responsibility
3. Responsible love and concern
4. Act as if
5. No free lunch
6. What goes on around shall come around
7. Trust your environment
8. Understand rather than be understood
9. It's better to give than receive
10. You cannot keep it unless you give it away

"No free lunch" refers to the principle that one gets nothing in Daytop without earning it. "What goes on around shall come around" means that however people in the house are treating others, they can expect similar treatment themselves eventually: if they are showing kindness, they can expect to receive this from others; if they are being selfish they can expect this response when they are looking for help. "You cannot keep it unless you give it away" refers to one's progress in Daytop and the good feelings that go with it. When a person tries to rest on his laurels and stops taking the trouble to help his fellows in Daytop, he slips backwards and loses his good feelings, because the very act of giving concern and help to others is something that he (and everyone) needs for their personal growth. The other items in the "Unwritten Philosophy" should be readily understood.

By the following summer (1968), the "Added Philosophy" had appeared as an addendum. Like its predecessor, its origin and authorship were not determined. A copy of the later document was found on the inside of the closet where service crew equipment was kept, presumably put there by a zealous department head. There it could be seen by most residents of the house who had to use this closet to get brooms, mops, dusters, etc., for the daily cleaning of their rooms. The Added Philosophy states:

1. To make it work you have to buy the whole package
2. If you want something you must work for it
3. Be careful what you ask for; you might get it
4. Awareness
5. Confrontation
6. No rewards for bad behavior

The first item "To make it work you have to buy the whole package" refers to the Daytop ideology or Concept. "Be careful what you ask for; you might get it" refers particularly to residents who ask for positions carrying a lot of status and responsibility in the house. They usually complain a lot when refused but occasionally an overambitious resident is taught a lesson and actually granted his wish in order to see if he really is ready to cope with such responsibilities.

SOCIAL ORGANIZATION

What does it take to make Daytop Village work? We can broaden our focus to ask: what are the fundamental requirements for any therapeutic community, defined as any group of people who come together in order to change their outlook and behavior and who go about this in a cooperative way?

A fundamental requirement for any therapeutic community is a structure of rules and role expectations that are capable of being conformed to to a high degree—given the nature of the recruits—and that provide or make possible some of the basic requirements of treatment (individual change in the desired direction). The specifics of this structure will vary from one therapeutic community to another, depending upon the nature of the recruits, their problems, the motivation they have to conform, and so forth. Underneath these variations there is a common set of requirements that must be met for the goals of a therapeutic community to be achievable.

These requirements can be ranked hierarchically on three levels: on level one are the most basic requirements for the survival of the individual members as living organisms—food, shelter, etc.; on the second level are the requirements for an organized social structure, so that this collection of organisms can form a cohesive and somewhat self-contained group or community; and on the third level are the requirements necessary for this group to achieve its collective goals, for it to be not just a community but a *therapeutic* community. It would be possible to subdivide level three into two distinct levels where one covered the requirements for goal attainment by *any* means and the second covered the requirements for goal attainment only by the ways defined in the particular community as normatively appropriate. For present purposes, though, we shall deal only with three levels altogether.

On level one, the basic requirements are for food, shelter, waste disposal, heating, and medical care. They may be supplied in kind by arrangement with government agencies or by soliciting donations from private sources. Again, these requirements may be met either directly, for example, by providing the use of housing ready for occupation, or indirectly, by providing materials and tools for group members to make their own facilities—by remodeling existing but unsuitable structures or even starting from scratch. In the latter case a further set of requirements is generated, namely the skill, manpower, and organization to convert those raw materials into the needed product. As an alternative to contributions in kind, support may be provided in cash which can be exchanged either for the actual requirements or (again) for the raw materials to be converted by the members' own efforts. At Daytop a combination of these approaches is found, with some of the requirements on this level being met by cash funds from governmental sources and some from private donations (mainly in kind).

In order to solicit and collect donations a further subsidiary level of requirements is generated—the need for telephone and other communication services and for transportation to collect donations. Thus part of the cash income of the group is invested in telephone and vehicle expenses in the hope of "hustling" greater quantities of basic requirements than purchasing directly by cash would provide.

On the second level are the requirements of organized group life. They include: a structure of positions or roles with agreed duties, so that members are fairly well aware of who is supposed to do what; a structure of authority, so that members know who is supposed to take orders from whom; a codifiable set of rules, so that the general expectations of conduct are comprehensible—including the procedures for finding out what to do when one does not know; methods for recruiting new members and teaching them the normative expectations of the group; communication mechanisms so that all members know what is going on in the group and in particular so that those members who have special responsibilities for enforcing norms know about incidents of nonconformity; and sanctions to discourage such deviance. We have discussed at some length the framework of organization and the mechanisms for enforcing norms in Daytop. Both, as we know, are highly developed.

In important ways the shape taken by the group's social structure (level two) depends upon the way first-level requirements are met. The more the labor of group members is used to fix up buildings, prepare food, and so forth, the more social relationships are structured along the lines of work-function in the house.

On the third level are the requirements of goal attainment. In the case of the therapeutic community this means bringing about individual changes in attitudes, values, and coping styles. Requirements on this level presuppose that those on the prior levels have been and are being met, just as second-level requirements presuppose the satisfaction of first-level requirements. On top of the requirements of biological survival and social organization, then, the attainment of therapeutic goals requires some additional processes to take place. Feedback on the interpersonal level is necessary so that each resident has his behavior mirrored to him by peers. He is judged in terms of Daytop values, and pressure is applied to make him improve. At Daytop this takes place both informally and formally, for example in encounter groups, in haircuts and other learning experiences, and, to some extent, in morning meeting. Communication mechanisms keeping staff adequately informed about the progress and problems of each resident are necessary, so that they are in a position to make appropriate therapeutic decisions for each one (job changes, learning experiences, privileges, etc.). Lastly, *treatment* in its more specific sense must be provided. This includes counseling in the one-to-one situation by staff and older residents who are specially trusted and the use of encounter groups for people to relate to feelings that are troubling them.

These three levels of functional requirements form a hierarchy in the sense that each depends on the fulfillment of the preceding level. It is also important to realize that certain features of the Daytop social structure serve the requirements of two or even three levels at once. The major example of this might be the fact that all negative sanctions in Daytop serve both to maintain a certain level of conformity or social control (level two) and to help residents to learn to control impulsive desires (level three, therapeutic goals). We shall now examine several features of the Daytop structure that are implicated in both level two (social control) and level three (therapy) functions, notably authority, the role of helpers, communication and controls, and the "act as if" principle.

Authority Authority resides mainly in a hierarchy of formal statuses based on the work structure: house directors, coordinators, heads of departments, and ramrods. Authority is also attached to seniority within Daytop; newer residents are supposed to respect more senior ones and comply with orders they may give. There are also some expectations (mainly tacit) governing the way younger residents may confront residents senior to them. It is maintained that *all* members of Daytop must be open to being challenged and confronted. It is also a point of criticism against a resident if he confines his pull-ups exclusively to those lower than himself ("easy shots"). However, someone who loudly "dumped" an older resident for a pull-up would be severely castigated, on the spot and again later in a formal haircut, for showing lack of respect for an older member. If the younger resident feels that the older one is hiding behind his status to avoid confrontation he has the usual recourse of taking him to a group. The outcome of that will depend on the line taken by the group leader. If the younger resident is still unsatisfied he can appeal to a house director. Seniority does not constitute a totally ascriptive base of status, however, for residents are sometimes formally deprived of their seniority as a result of misconduct. A resident who splits from the house reenters at the bottom of the seniority ladder again, though he may be awarded his "time" back after proving himself worthy of it.

Elders and Peers as Helpers Of course, Daytop residents know that the authority figures in the house have power and privileges and that they think and act differently from themselves in very important ways. They are held in respect for all these reasons. Yet, compared to any conventional psychiatric, correctional, or rehabilitation agency, the distinctions between staff and clients are remarkably small. The visitor to Daytop cannot readily tell who is staff and who is not until he asks. Daytop residents see these authority figures as being significantly different from authority figures they have met in other situations. They are "open" and "loose" rather than "closed" and "rigid." They do not stand on ceremony with people, and they are open to being challenged and to listening to grievances against the program and staff without feeling threatened. They are ready to talk about themselves as well as listen sympathetically to a resident who wants to talk to them about his problems. Thus an identification develops between resident and staff member across the existing authority gap. This identification process is one of the crucial factors in the success of Daytop as a therapeutic community.

Interviews with graduates indicate that there is another crucial factor in the process of personal change in Daytop—also on the one-to-one level of interaction. This factor is a relationship with a few peers based on mutual trust and responsible concern. In spite of the fact that residents can identify with Daytop authority figures to a remarkable degree, there is still a small but significant gap in that relationship. When relating to one's peers, however, that gap can be completely eliminated. As Richie Rode explains,

> I think everybody picks out a couple of people that they like. Usually you're closer to your peers in the beginning because you can identify with them the most. They kinda feel the way that you do. The other [older] people are telling you how you should feel but what comes across is that they don't really *feel* the way you feel. They haven't used drugs for about a year and they're on a different level as far as you're concerned. They can identify with your feelings because they used to feel that way but the impression that you get is that they don't feel that way any more because they're acting and talking a lot different from the way you feel . . . plus they also represent authority. That's something that's gonna get you uptight . . . [although] you do see that they're not acting like authority figures anywhere else.

This close relationship that can exist between peers in Daytop is only positive and therapeutic as long as the parties act with responsible concern toward each other. More typically in schools, mental hospitals, and prisons, peer groups function mainly to undermine the official goals of the organization. In Daytop, however, we have seen that there are mechanisms whereby staff keep control over informal groups to ensure that they do not function in a negative manner. These mechanisms are important not just because of the socialization effect but rather because they create a context in which the efforts of individuals to help themselves have a maximum chance of success.

Communication and Controls There are various formal arrangements ensuring fast and accurate communication. Communication *upward* in the status structure will be considered first. Every resident must check in and out of the building. During working hours he must inform his superior and colleagues of his whereabouts and activities in a very comprehensive manner. (Permission is necessary for many things, too.) When he sees a fellow resident acting strangely he must inform a senior person, who will convey the message to the coordinator on duty as well as speak to the resident in question. Every department head makes weekly written attitude reports on his workers and his coordinator makes reports on him.

Each day the directors meet with the coordinators to review matters. These may be technical problems of work that require the cooperation of several departments, or authorization for some new policy, or they may be therapeutic problems, such as the request of some individual for a job change or a privilege (such as a visit to his home), or the problems a coordinator is having in coping with an unresponsive member of his department. Sometimes, too, the personal problems of coordinators are discussed, either because the individual having the problem brings it up, or because his seniors do so, or because it emerges from other problems under discussion. Social control, therapy for residents, and therapy-cum-training for staff and incipient staff are thus all intimately related.

Communication *down* the status hierarchy operates mainly through a variety of meetings. Every day begins with morning meeting for the whole house. When an especially serious infraction is discovered, a general meeting will be called, breaking into the day's routine. This is done in order to bring the infraction to the attention of the whole house and for sentiments of strong disapproval to be ritually expressed.

Feedback on the individual level is recognized to be of paramount importance in this therapeutic community. The shaming of an individual in front of his peers is a weighty form of feedback for that individual, of course. More important in terms of frequency, though, is informal confrontation. Confronting and being confronted are central to Daytop treatment and to social control in this community.

Pull-ups are made constantly throughout the day. Residents must learn to accept them and to learn from them; they must also learn to give them. Much of the feedback, involving constant surveillance of residents by each other, that is so important for both social control and for treatment, operates through pull-ups.

Confrontation throughout the day is a most important part of treatment in Daytop. Encounter groups also provide an important part of treatment in a formally structured setting. Two main functions are served by groups: they provide for controlled release of hostility and verbal aggression, and they are the setting for confrontation with intense social pressures for honesty and change.

Confrontation has been mentioned many times in this account of life in Daytop, since it is a pervasive and characteristic feature. This is very different from what commonly happens in other known social groups in Western society. In these groups, very often the person who acts in violation of group norms is shunned, ignored, and/or made the target of private ridicule behind his back. Only rarely will he be directly confronted by his fellows and told what it is they disapprove of —sometimes he will not know what he is doing wrong and hence will be unable, even though willing, to mend his ways. He is pressured out of the group or at least made to withdraw from the mainstream of activities. At the same time he withdraws into himself, becoming less and less attuned to social cues and hence progressively more deviant and more rejected. In Daytop, though, confrontation does not entail rejection; and withdrawal, far from being expected, is against the norms and will itself lead to a confrontation ("How come you're isolating yourself from everyone?").

The mechanisms through which social control is maintained in Daytop are at once its most crucial and most impressive features. In describing the various facets of the structure, we were describing patterns of behavior and normative expectations that are in remarkable harmony with each other. We now have to try to explain how this is possible—this high level of conformity to an unusually stringent set of norms by people formerly characterized by extremely uncontrolled behavior.

In analyzing social groups we normally speak of positive and negative sanctions or rewards and punishments. At Daytop the word "punishment" is most carefully avoided and all negative sanctions are defined as "learning experiences." Each one is supposed to be tailored to the nature of his problem and its whole purpose (he is told) is to help him improve, not to punish him.

One reward is promotion to more responsible jobs within the house. Job status carries general status and respect and job demotion (which is not at all infrequent) is one of the most severe learning experiences. On entering Daytop, a resident gives up many rights that are taken for granted outside. These become privileges that can be earned back by good conduct. Much staff time is taken up in deciding on these requests.

Negative sanctions are easy to see and many have already been discussed in Chapter Four. There are pull-ups from individual fellow residents; for more serious offenses, a haircut group will be convened. The effect on the deviant himself seems to be strong but we should not forget about the effects on those who give out the punishment. It is very hard for them, especially for the friends of the deviant, but it helps them reject that part of their former selves that they see in the deviant. These learning experiences may seem severe by the standards of outside society, but they are only used after gentler methods have proven insufficient.

The novice in his first month is discouraged from talking too much to other novices, lest they reinforce each others' negative attitudes and tend to form a group of deviants within the house. New residents who knew each other on the street will be forbidden to fraternize at all for a time. Those who are not yet ready for the commitment to Daytop values must not be allowed to form deviant groups that would hold them back from developing such a commitment. At the same time, the older members are going out of their way to "pull in" the newcomers, to be friendly to them, acquaint them with the ways of Daytop, and talk over problems. This is how Daytop on the whole avoids the traditional staff-inmate dichotomy.

Act As If A basic requirement made explicit to residents is always to act as if you were the kind of person you want to be, even though you know inside yourself that this is not the real you—yet. By doing this consistently, they are told, you will gradually come to think and feel the way you are acting and thus *become* that kind of person. Clearly, if most of Daytop's residents are following the "act as if" rule, the level of conformity to rules of conduct and the extent of verbal affirmation of Daytop values that we have observed exceeds the level of internal commitment. These people are not as committed as they appear; to a great extent they are presenting a concerted *act as if.*

Let us consider the implications of this for the process of resocialization and personal change. Let us assume that a given resident is acting as if and, slowly building up a personal investment in change for himself. He is developing his commitment to this new pattern. Meanwhile his fellow residents are mostly acting as if, while some of them are really committed. He does not know which is which unless he gets to know these individuals very well indeed. So he tends to take them at face value. The atmosphere at Daytop is thus one in which acceptance of the official norms and values is assumed and open rebellion nonexistent. In one sense the resident has no choice but to take his fellows at face value, because a major part of their "act as if" consists of making pull-ups on him when his "act as if" is not good enough. And these pull-ups and other negative sanctions that may be invoked in support of them are real enough—even if the person instigating them is merely *acting* the role of a committed Daytop resident. Conversely, the resident who serves as the subject of our example demonstrates his "act as if" by pulling-up other residents. Residents do this because they are eventually rewarded for it with privileges and promotions to higher status jobs. More immediate rewards are general approbation, and not being pulled-up and confronted as much themselves. Also residents find that they get good feelings and begin to feel like part of the Daytop community as a result of consistent conformity and a developing identification with its values and its leaders.

A similar process operates in relation to the teaching function within Daytop. Every resident is supposed to be "giving away what he has got," that is, teaching those newer than himself what he knows about Daytop, its procedures and principles, especially the business of personal growth. Much of the "data" that is taught may consist of beliefs and attitudes only superficially held by the teacher, but it can still benefit the recipient and he can in turn pass it on to yet newer residents. Again, we can trace the same process in the way residents "elaborate" upon pull-ups in morning meeting. Those who elaborate are not supposed to be completely cured people who never make mistakes themselves. Anyone can elaborate, though in practice it is mostly the older residents who do so.

Turning to haircuts and other learning experiences, we find that Daytop policy is to involve residents in these quite early in their careers. Perhaps in his first few weeks a resident will be called in to participate in a haircut, where he is expected to join in shouting abuse at a fellow resident for his bad behavior. Someone who had received a lot of haircuts himself in those first few weeks would probably not be brought in to help give one, but no one escapes without some haircuts. It is not at all unknown for a resident to help give a haircut one day, and receive one himself the next day.

Someone who has shouted harsh words at another for his stupid behavior can hardly sit down with him later and commiserate over the injustice of his treatment. It is extremely hard to play one's part in a haircut. If it is not done in the approved way, pull-ups will be made at the end of the haircut when the subject himself has left. Taking part in this ritual on the side of authority helps in developing commitment to Daytop norms and values. In the short term it is more significant in relation to social control.

The importance of the "act as if" policy can be underlined by referring back to the seniority structure of the house. As we saw in chapter one, the residents of eighteen months and over constitute only 29 percent of the Staten Island house. Even assuming that all of these older residents were mature and committed to Daytop values, they could probably not ensure a therapeutic environment without massive support from other residents. As we have pointed out, the fact that a particular resident gives help to other residents in no way conflicts with the fact that he needs the help of others himself. Indeed, it is a fundamental assumption at Daytop that this *must* happen.

How can this policy of "act as if" be reconciled with the great emphasis on honesty that we discussed earlier? On "public" occasions, for example in morning meeting, or when making pull-ups "on the floor" (around the house), or when teaching newer residents, the requirement of "act as if" applies. In encounter groups, however, or when discussing personal problems with an older resident, complete honesty is required. This, from my observation, is the separation that operates and it seems to be a viable one.

To some, the "act as if" policy may seem like hypocrisy and the worst kind of phoniness. There is an important distinction, to be made, however. In one kind of situation A pretends to B that he (A) holds a high opinion of B or of something B has done, in order to gain some influence over B. In the other kind of situation (the one we find in Daytop) A wants to change himself and acts as if the change were already made. The aim of this pretense is not to manipulate B but to help A to make the change in reality. In the first example, A is representing himself as holding views that he does not hold and never intends or wishes to really hold; in the second example, A is hoping and striving to become the kind of person he represents himself as. While the first situation can legitimately be called hypocrisy, I do not think the second can be regarded as such.

TWO FACES AND TWO PHASES

Early in our first chapter we noted the surface impression that visitors typically get on first visits to Daytop. These were described as essentially two-fold: orderliness and discipline on the one hand, and warmth and comradeliness on the other hand. Upon further extended visits and periods in residence, together with attempts to analyze my developing perceptions, I came to sharpen and refine these early impressions but never did abandon them. Instead I came more and more to view Daytop as having two sides to it, two "faces" which were sharply different from each other. And I came to believe that the essential character and effectiveness of Daytop derived precisely from this combination of two complementary opposites.

The success of Daytop, not only in terms of social control but also in terms of personality change, is achieved with a sample of former addicts whose representativeness of the larger universe of addicts is unknown. And it is achieved with the help of a high level of selectivity. Nevertheless it should be conceded that this achievement is a remarkable one. In Daytop former drug addicts who lived only for the next fix are changing themselves, with each other's help, into people who not only can live without drugs but who are learning new ways of coping with life and its emotional stresses. We have analyzed many of the features of the social organization of Daytop and how they affect the process of social learning. Now we wish to emphasize that Daytop incorporates two quite different types of learning situations, which we will call "the two faces of Daytop."

The two faces can be defined as follows: one features disclipline and conformity; the other, mutual concern among members and the warmth of a close, fraternal group. On one level perhaps it may seem that these two faces are in conflict with each other, and though there are indeed strains, they complement each other in fundamentally important ways. Concern and warmth for each other, without an underlying awareness of the difficult job to be done and the need to insist that one's peers live up to the standards which are demanded in the group and which are necessary for their own development, could not lead to basic changes of attitude and behavior patterns. At the same time, discipline and the rigid enforcement of rules without the awareness of warmth and real concern from those enforcing the rules and handing out the sanctions, would not be accepted by those receiving them. In other words, warmth without discipline would be comfortable but not effective resocialization; and discipline without warmth would produce an empty house from which all residents had left in disgust; or (under special circumstances) it might result in a highly coercive organization which would be quite ineffective at resocialization.

The discipline face of Daytop may be seen most clearly in the work situation, though it is by no means confined to this part of the day. At work the resident is in a precise position in an authority structure, with individuals placed above him and having the authority to give him orders which he must obey. He may suggest a better way of doing the job but if his superior does not wish to hear it he must follow his orders. He has the right (and obligation) to confront the superior outside of the work situation and to deal with his resentment towards him in an encounter group, but for now he must do as he is told without complaint. In the event that a resident had a boss who consistently refused to listen to his ideas when his own were unsuccessful, confrontation in the approved manner would lead to the boss being required by *his* boss to change his ways. In this setting residents in Daytop are not dealing with each other as individual people but as functionaries within a bureaucratic structure. They are learning to operate within situations defined by norms of universalism, achievement, functional specificity, and affective neutrality.

The other face of Daytop is one where residents are interacting as individuals learning to appreciate themselves and others for their unique qualities as people, and striving to grow and help each other to grow, through mutual confrontation. In the encounter group setting we see this most clearly. There we see that many of the restrictions of the work situation are dropped: anger can be expressed—as can any feeling—and seniority is no protection. At the same time this is not a permissive situation, for the normative limits are very clearly stated and sternly enforced. One person speaks at a time, no one moves from his seat, and so forth.

Although we characterized the work situation as being almost totally a bureaucratic and impersonal one, it would not be true to characterize groups as the exact opposite—expressing fraternal concern and nothing more. For although this concern plays a large part in what transpires in the group, it is supposed to be a *responsible* concern—that is, a concern informed and guided by an awareness of the long-term changes one's fellow must go through in coming to terms with his reality. When the group is focused on confronting an individual member with his behavior, this is very clear. But also when the group's focus is on opening up a member to areas of his emotions of which he is not aware, they are doing the same thing—unavoidably hurting him in order to help him in the long-term process of growth and change.

These aspects of the normative role of the helper in the group situation do not differ materially from the role which is expected of a Daytop member at all times, whether it is in helping to administer a haircut, making a pull-up around the house, sitting down and talking with another resident or in any other situation. The expectation is that he extend not just concern but *responsible* concern. And showing responsible concern is always harder for a person than giving indulgent concern, that is, short-term emotional support or "giving him what he wants."

Returning to our image of the two faces of Daytop, we may label one as the "Hard" face and the other as the "Soft-Hard" face. Given the duality of the latter it could not properly be called simply the "soft face."

We may state formally the conditions associated with these two "faces" or types of socialization setting in the diagram on page 115.

To clarify one point, the "soft-hard" setting includes both the one-to-one conversations and the institutionalized encounter group meetings. In both cases the individuals are relating to each other as persons, not just in terms of their roles in relation to some task or in terms of their respective positions in the work structure. The interaction may be and commonly is loaded with affectivity (feelings)

TABLE 1 TWO TYPES OF SOCIALIZATION SETTING

	The "Hard" Setting	*The "Soft-Hard" Setting*
NATURE OF RULES	Extensive, detailed rules; substantive in nature (as opposed to procedural).	Fewer rules; procedural. A few principles of conduct, but wide-ranging and considered very important.
SANCTIONS FOR BREACH OF RULES	Quick and fairly stern; fairly frequently issued.	Quick and very stern; rarely issued.
MAIN FUNCTION OF SETTING	Training in conformity, self-control, various skills; learning self-respect.	Exploration of psychodynamics and restructuring them.
NATURE OF SOCIAL RELATIONS	Mainly impersonal, task-oriented; obedience to superior demanded.	Personal, oriented to general patterns of behavior and attitude; hierarchical ranks are no bar to expression of feelings and confrontation.

whereas in the hard setting it is supposed to be under control ("affectively neutral"). Although, as we noted earlier, work has important therapeutic implications in Daytop, during work there is no discussion of personal problems or "relating" as such. If a person asks for permission to do this because he is feeling under a lot of strain—more than he feels he can handle—this must be considered time out of work and not part of the same setting.

While conformity is the essence of the hard setting and learning impulse control and "toughening your belly" are among its prime goals, in the case of the soft-hard setting the goal is to bring the individual into a true existential encounter with himself and his reality (through his encounter with others who relate to him in a responsible manner). What we mean by this ponderous phrase "existential encounter" is that the individual takes the responsibility for looking at the kind of person he really is now and at his ideals for the future. And, most important, he takes responsibility for changing his behavior or style of life accordingly. Yet this definition makes it sound too rational a process and ignores the intensely emotional side of getting oneself to this point—the terrible fears of making the commitment and of failing, the poignancy of aspirations so deeply held, the anger and resentment at those who try to help, which has to be vented but eventually gives way to feelings of love which are both painful and ecstatic. Through the soft-hard settings the individual comes to terms with himself, begins to define a new self, and assumes the responsibility for making it come into being.

Through this process ideally the individual internalizes the values of Daytop and integrates them into his inner self. On this basis he should have more success in actualizing these values after he leaves Daytop than the person who has just gone through the motions of "act as if," conforming to the hard settings alone. That kind of resident—and they do exist, or course—is very successful in the house but when he must cope with unfamiliar situations, without either the guidance or the surveillance he was accustomed to in Daytop, the "act as if" resident is more likely to slip back into old patterns, not necessarily into drug use (though this is one possibility), but into lying, cheating, manipulating, or some other form of "dope-fiend behavior."

For the treatment of drug addicts and character-disordered persons, I believe that the most important requirement of a therapeutic community is that it *combine* within the same organization *both* hard and soft-hard settings. The coexistence of two very different settings implies that institutional provisions must be made for differentiating the two types of situation and making it quite clear when each set of expectations is operative. In Daytop this is mainly institutionalized through "groups" and the procedure of "dropping slips," and through the less formalized procedure of sitting down with a more senior resident in order to talk over some personal problem. At these times it is clear that the soft-hard situation obtains. When two residents sit down to "relate" the situation is the same. Most other times, at work in the house, in seminar, morning meeting, the situation is usually "hard."

At the same time, it is important that when someone has made himself liable to sanctions for violating the rules of either type of learning situation, they are not dealt with in an entirely mechanical or impersonal fashion. While the administration of a haircut or a conventional "learning experience" is commonly quite mechanical and stereotyped, after it is over the person who received it can talk to any of those who gave it to him person-to-person. Thus, the haircut represents a "hard" situation but the "patch-up" or later talk sessions are "soft-hard" in our present terminology.

The importance of keeping such a balance when administering negative sanctions is strongly emphasized by Richie Rode, who formerly worked as a Daytop staff member. He uses the example of a resident being given a sign to wear.

> The person who puts that sign around his neck has to understand what he's doing. His attitude has to be not that this kid is being punished, but that he is being put in a position to look at something so that he can learn from this experience. The second step is that he makes sure that the people within the environment, the residents and the rest of the staff give him the proper concern—keeping an eye on him if he looks uptight, taking him off his job and sitting down and talking with him, and also when he goes into a group really let him have it and really make him live up to his responsibilities. And usually if all that happens the person will begin to accept the situation. It's very important that the balance is met between trying to discipline him for what he did wrong and at the same time having an understanding of his feelings—showing him that we all understand the way he's feeling. If he's just given a sign and then neglected—and nobody pulls him in on that level—there's a good chance that he'll feel he's really getting screwed. The important thing is that that balance is there—that you have both.

We may look at Daytop as having two faces, as in the foregoing analysis; at the same time we may look at it as having two complementary *phases* in the typical Daytop career.

In Daytop, phase one is characterized by the relative predominance of the hard face (though the soft-hard one is there too) and phase two is characterized by the opposite: predominance of the soft-hard face, with the hard one in a secondary position. In phase one the emphasis is on learning to conform to the many rules of the house, to control one's impulses and not react when one gets upset, to perform in various areas, such as making pull-ups, speaking in morning meeting and seminars, pulling in newer residents, using groups in the approved way, doing a good job in one's work assignments, and so forth. In phase two these same requirements are in effect but it is taken for granted that the resident is meeting them. Now emphasis shifts to the area of dealing with one's feelings effectively, learning to seek help when difficulty arises instead of waiting to be confronted about it after the fact, learning to distinguish readily between "gut" feeling and "intellectual" thinking, learning to take a proper pride in one's achievements, and developing a reasoned understanding of why one holds the Daytop values which he is coming to adopt as his own. Briefly, in phase two it is the exploration of one's own psychodynamics that is emphasized, whereas phase one is to a large extent "act as if."

In phase one, the resident is learning to operate within the restricted but demanding environment of Daytop; in phase two he is learning to cope with living under less rigid and less comprehensive controls and also with the more complex and confusing, less supervised environment of outside society. That is, in the latter phase, one is tentatively exploring the outside environment and, in so doing, testing out the strength of what one learned in the first phase. The intensive exploration of psychodynamics goes hand in hand with this, as new situations and their stresses give rise to emotional reactions in the individual which he sometimes cannot handle and hence brings in for discussion. These reactions throw more light on the nature of his personality than he would get just continuing to operate in the same, restricted environment of the group.

In Daytop there is no explicit concept of two phases, or, for that matter, *any* number of phases in the treatment process. The closest thing to this would be the concept of "humps." As mentioned earlier, these define certain crises in the individual's personal development in Daytop, whereas the notion of the two phases focuses more on a shift in the expectations placed upon the individual in Daytop. As he moves from the notional phase one gradually into phase two, Daytop staff revise their expectations of him upwards and they modify his environment by allowing him more privileges and diminishing the external restraints upon him. This enables them to see to what extent he has really internalized his learning and if he can apply it in situations where he has to use his own judgment. Since no one in Daytop thinks in terms of a two-phase concept there cannot be an abrupt and official change of status from phase one to phase two. Rather there is a gradual change in the way staff define their expectations for individual residents as they evaluate their progress. Such shifts in staff thinking commonly occur when job changes are to be made. Residents are usually made aware of these re-evaluations through individual talks with staff members.

As has already been stated, I believe that the combination of the two distinct types of learning situations within Daytop accounts in large measure for its relatively high degree of success. The two-phase notion now extends this proposition further. I maintain that it is necessary to distinguish between these two phases, their differing functions and requirements, and to appreciate that the first phase must be satisfactorily completed before the second can be successful. (This theory is developed more fully in relation to other socializing agencies including schools in Sugarman, 1973.)

8 / Crisis and continuity

In the previous seven chapters we have looked at Daytop as a self-contained community, with only fleeting reference to its relationship to the outside society. This larger system in which Daytop exists can be forgotten or taken for granted only as long as certain conditions continue to be met. As long as they are met, Daytop remains in equilibrium with the larger system and its internal operation can continue undisturbed. What then are these conditions?

Daytop depends on a continuous flow of funds from various government sources in order to pay rent and salaries, purchase food and other supplies, and pay for telephones, light, heat, and other necessary services. It depends on a flow of new prospects seeking admission and meeting the admission criteria, to replace those who split and those who complete the program and leave. It depends on a minimum level of community acceptance, so that at least residents are not harassed and preferably are treated with some civility by neighbors and local tradespeople, and so that deliverymen are not afraid to call at the house. It depends on visitors coming to Open House, so that some therapeutic interaction may take place with "straight people." It depends on some of the businesses which are approached by community relations department "hustlers" being willing to make donations of goods, for the psychological good of these residents as well as for the economic good of the house.

Among the more remote conditions on which the equilibrium of Daytop as we have seen it is dependent is the continued existence of statutes making heroin use and the use of certain other drugs illegal, the dependence of the addict on black-market sources of supply, the efforts of law enforcement agents to interfere with the supply of illegal drugs (thereby raising prices), and the efforts of illegal suppliers to keep their trade profitable. All of these factors combine to make the life of the addict hard because of the difficulty of evading the police and of raising the large sum of money needed for each day's supply of drugs. Because the life of the addict is so hard in contemporary America—in particular because of the real danger of being sent to jail for long periods of time—some are willing to accept the terms of admission to Daytop. If these conditions were to change—if heroin and other drugs of addiction were made legal and supplies became available at much lower prices—then the demand for admission to Daytop and the willingness to stay there could be expected to diminish greatly, possibly vanishing altogether.

Daytop can continue to operate the way we found it in 1967 and 1968, as long as these various conditions relating to the larger society and the relationship between Daytop and that society remain unchanged. If any of those major conditions were to change, though, the internal life of Daytop may have to change as a result. Conversely, any major change *inside* Daytop may produce changes in its relations with the larger system. Such a change did occur. It was under way in 1968 and continued into 1969. This change, which was to have profound consequences for Daytop and its residents, involved a redefinition by Deitch and his staff of the goals and objectives of the community, a radicalization of its goals to embrace wide aims of challenging and attempting to change many aspects of the institutional structure of American society. Deitch and his close colleagues came to see Daytop as a movement for social change in America. This resulted in strained relations with the lay board of directors, legally empowered to make Daytop policy and to hire and fire staff. Both sides refused to compromise and the conflict polarized. After much suffering by Daytop residents and staff, a new equilibrium was reached with the board more powerful than before *vis-à-vis* the executive director and staff, and with a narrower and less radical definition of the community's goals in effect. We turn now to examine in more detail how this upheaval developed and, in so doing, to see some other dimensions of the life of this remarkable community.

So far our description and analysis of the Daytop way of life has been set in the "historical present," written from the perspective of an observer collecting data in 1967 and 1968. So far, then, we have mostly presented a picture of Daytop at just one phase of its development, alluding only quite briefly to the first year and the problems experienced in getting Daytop set on the course on which we found it in 1967 and 1968. At the end of 1968 and into 1969 certain developments known as "the big split" occurred, profoundly affecting Daytop as an organization and involving the sudden departure of David Deitch with most of his staff and most of the residents. We shall outline the main events in "the big split" and attempt to explain how it came about in terms of certain tensions and conflicts inherent in the relationship between Daytop, the closed community as we have seen it so far, and the larger system in which it exists, and in particular the relationship between Deitch and the lay board of directors of Daytop Village, Inc. In order to trace this development we shall change from the historical present tense to the past tense, as we assume the perspective of the present and look back over that sequence of events from today's viewpoint. As we do this, we move for the first time from studying the internal workings of Daytop to look at some aspects of its relationship with the larger system around it.

DAYTOP WIDENS ITS SCOPE

Daytop Lodge began as a project in corrections or rehabilitation—a small but ambitious pilot project involving twenty-five residents initially. That was in 1963. Five years later, in 1968, the number of residents had increased to some two-hundred fifty, a tenfold increase. And it was to go higher yet. Ambitious as the initial project was, it is very doubtful that any of its initial sponsors could have conceived just how much that small project would grow—not just in size but in scope.

Daytop expanded beyond the initial conception of a program only for probationers to include volunteers and other applicants with other forms of legal constraints on them. It expanded to take in women and dependent children as well as males, as in the initial scheme. It became an independent incorporated body instead of just an operation within the Probation Department. Most significantly of all, under the vision and leadership of David Deitch, Daytop's objectives became radically redefined.

Daytop came to be defined by its leaders more as a social movement with radical or perhaps utopian goals and less as a mere rehabilitation program. The very word "program" became anathema as applied to Daytop. No longer would Daytop staff see their function as "rehabilitating" drug addicts in order to return them to society to play the part of conforming citizens—as a kind of "first-aid station" dealing with the casualties of a dangerous but acceptable game. Daytop leaders came to reject the idea that the values of mainstream American society were basically sound and that their main task was to prepare former addicts to return, drug-free, to that society.

Under Deitch's influences, Daytop staff came to take the view that Daytop stood for *better* values, and they felt they upheld these values with far more integrity than did the typical representatives of secular American society. In Daytop people were learning to live by the values of honesty in personal relationships, concern for each other, responsibility in accepting the consequences of one's actions, and working for what one wants.

While most Americans might claim to uphold the same values, in practice they give them at best second place to their preoccupation with material acquisition, the preservation of their comfortable *status quo*, the display of status symbols, and the quest for power. In the emergent Daytop view, emanating from Deitch, the stress imposed on people by the rat race and false values of American society, the lack of community, the prejudice, hate, and fear, and the corruption of public institutions all were seen as contributing importantly to the residents' earlier fall into addiction. This was not held to remove the blame or responsibility from them, as emphasized in the traditional prospect interview. It was, however, seen as a vitally important factor to be taken into account when planning a long-term attack on the drug problem from a preventive approach. If the causes of drug addiction lie even partly in social, economic, and political institutions, placing intolerable stresses on individuals and warping their growth, then the only way to curb the incidence of addiction is by reforming and changing those social, economic, and political institutions.

Nor are drug addicts held to be the only victims or products of this rotten society. Not only drug addicts, criminals, delinquents, and character-disordered persons, but others too are counted among the moral cripples produced by this society. All who fail to live up to the Daytop ideal of confronting the reality of what they are and reality of the situation in which they find themselves, of having the honesty to decide what they really want out of life and the courage to make those changes which may be necessary, all these are seen as cripples equally with the drug addict. Many of these "cripples" are apparently respectable and responsible people who, on the surface, take care of their material responsibilities to their families but who are not open and honest in their relationships with their friends, parents, spouse, and others.

In other words, Daytop people were urged to view themselves not as half-mended cripples of uncertain worth, struggling to be accepted back into the world of the healthy, but as one-time moral cripples who have been ennobled by their successful struggle and hence are now better than the average person. Deitch saw Daytop as a missionary center reaching out to save the souls of a certain subgroup of those in need of salvation (drug addicts) and aiming to send those it had saved back into the society that produced them (and all the other cripples with symptoms other than drugs) in order to try to change some of those conditions. Just as drug addiction was seen as only one symptom of an underlying personality problem, so from another point of view drug addiction in society was seen as a symptom of a basic pathology in social institutions.

Synanon, the organization on which Daytop was modeled, also takes the position that modern American society is basically not a good place to live. Their policy is to create their own subculture or subsociety in which people can live by the values of "the Concept" with others who want to do likewise, turning their backs on the rest of the population. It is perhaps not entirely correct to say that Synanon turns its back completely on the outside society, for their procurement teams or "hustlers" are extremely active in soliciting donations from individuals and businesses, and various Synanon industries are designed to make money from the outside population in order to provide for the material needs of Synanon. Until very recently Synanon received no support at all from government funds which means that their acquisitive activities have to be very energetic. Still more important, it means that Synanon is not legally responsible to anyone other than the board of directors of the Synanon Foundation, all hand-picked by the founder himself and all supporters of his ideas.

The situation at Daytop was significantly different and led eventually to conflict and a profound upheaval (the "big split"). The Daytop board of directors predated Deitch and apparently he made no effort to control it. Nor did he pay much attention to its directives.

These directors were quite different from the "corporation directors" appointed by David Deitch as senior members of his own staff. The board of directors was headed by a Catholic priest prominent in the ecclesiastical hierarchy of New York City (Msgr. William B. O'Brien) and included various business people and public figures. Among them was Dr. Daniel Casriel, holding the title of "Medical-Psychiatric Superintendant."

THE CONFLICT DEVELOPS

Deitch's attitude to the board apparently was to ignore it whenever it expressed a collective view at odds with his own. Legally the board was responsible for the conduct of Daytop and answerable for whatever took place in the Daytop houses.

Hence they disliked Deitch's independence or "arrogance," quite apart from the personal feelings of annoyance at having their views ignored.

Casriel, O'Brien, and other board members objected to some of Deitch's policies, in particular the radical turn of his social criticism and political philosophy and especially the fact that he preached these views to a very captive audience of ex-addicts, most of them in the very early stages of getting themselves straight and all subject to the very comprehensive system of social controls which we have described. Deitch's response to them was that if they wanted to influence Daytop policy they should "get involved" in the house and do so from within, not by passing motions at long-range. "This is our house and our community," he said, basing on this his moral claim to resist "outside interference."

A taste of Deitch's "social change" rhetoric and his emerging conception of Daytop's role in the world which he would preach in occasional speeches to house meetings may be conveyed by the following extracts taken from a speech he delivered in the summer of 1968. The occasion was the departure of a team of staff and residents to open a new Daytop house in New Haven, Connecticut. The quotations come from a tape recording of the speech.

> . . . our real job ain't got nothing to do with just overcoming drugs. Our real job . . . is confronting a racist community and challenging them to live the life we show by example. Our real job is to take those isolated neighborhoods and try to change them into communities . . . Now that scares a lot of people, but it's time you really understood. There are those of you in this house right now who are along for a free ride because you don't give a good Goddam about changing the world, the society in which we live, all the crap that's wrong in it—making it better. You only care about yourself. Me. Getting over dope. It's time for you to snap that the only reason Daytop works is because it is *not* concerned with "overcoming drug addiction." It's concerned with social change. . .
>
> Those of you who really *feel* the love in Daytop, start wondering about the fact that if you're just involved for the free ride how you can continue to want love and say you're giving it when you're not really plugged in to what we're doing.

While he speaks the audience is absolutely silent, apart from occasional coughs. There is no applause; there are no sounds of approbation or dissent—utter silence.

The moves and counter-moves, accusations, rebuttals and counter-accusations between the two sides built up as the conflict moved toward its *dénouement* late in 1968. "The Daytop Explosion" was the title of a long article in the *Village Voice* of November 21, 1968, with the subtitle "Addiction to Power." The author of this article, Joe Pilati, wrote, "Power is a drug too. All of the antagonists in last week's controversy surrounding Daytop Village . . . knew this to be the case. They disagree only on the crucial question of which side is obsessed with manipulation, in contrast to the side of the selfless therapeutic angels." The conflict was essentially one over power and who should control Daytop policy, with the specific accusations and "issues" as quite secondary epiphenomena.

For the record, the main accusations against Deitch were, in the words attributed to the board majority leaders by Pilati, that he and "his puppets . . . ensnared Daytop in a web of fiscal mismanagement, new left politicking, nepotism and general irresponsibility." Further specific charges were that an American flag was desecrated by being worn at a Daytop costume party, that Deitch had ignored board directives, and that paper work required by state funding agencies was not being done by Daytop staff. Deitch and his supporters denied the substance of all these allegations: the flag desecration never took place (though it was contemplated and discussed), the paper work was being done though slowly, directives were not ignored, three Deitch relatives by marriage were hired at Daytop but under justifiable circumstances and at lower salaries than they had been receiving formerly.

As for the accusation of "new left politicking," this was perhaps the most emotionally salient point of opposition for Deitch's enemies. It was linked, emotionally at least, to the charge of flag desecration, to the point that Deitch owned a Che Guevara poster (as well as many other posters of public figures, he pointed out), and that Daytop had invited a Black Panther speaker on one occasion. Our description of Daytop living patterns has already made it clear that they are and have always been highly communal in nature; but in the emotional atmosphere that built up around this dispute and power struggle, the simple fact of having a communal kitchen and living arrangements could be presented by the anti-Deitch party as a fact having sinister political implications.

Deitch's accusations against his board critics repeated the claim that they wanted to have control without any involvement in Daytop and hence without any knowledge of what it is all about. More specifically, his accusations as quoted in the *New York Post* for November 21, 1968, were that:

> The governing board wants us to make Daytop a factory. They want to push addicts in and then crank them out in a prescribed amount of time. This doesn't work. There is no such thing as a rehabilitation factory or assembly line. It takes time to rehabilitate an addict.

O'Brien, quoted in the same newspaper article, claimed that this was a misunderstanding and that the board wanted only to ensure "accountability," not to "take over the running of Daytop."

THE BIG SPLIT

As the dispute worked up to its peak, Deitch fired seven staff members who agreed with the board and opposed him. Shortly after, Deitch submitted his resignation to the board, along with the resignations of the sixty-one staff members. These "resignations" did not mean that they were leaving their positions, however, but that they were planning to continue without pay and without accepting any vestige of remaining obligation to the board. Staff members who were not already living in the house, moved in and all began a "sit in" policy in defiance of the board.

"We're going to stay here, because we live here and this is our community," said Deitch. "Our resignation was from the board, not from the community. We will not voluntarily leave our house and our community."

They knew that the board would cut off funds, for they had threatened to do so and they did. The defiant staff were not in immediate trouble on that account, though, for they had reserves of food and other supplies in stock and had drawn cash in anticipation from the Daytop bank accounts before they were frozen by the board. More serious was the other weapon remaining to the board, that of eviction. Legally the staff who had resigned had no right to remain on Daytop premises if the board wanted them out, as indeed it did. Deitch and his supporters thought and hoped that the board would shrink from so drastic a step, since it meant in effect evicting not only the staff but the residents (and some dependent children) too. In theory the residents could have stayed and waited for the board to send in replacement staff but board spokesmen had no access to residents to make offers to them or explain their position. They heard only from David Deitch and the staff members who supported him. The seven staff members opposing him who were fired were known derisively as "splittees." Some residents did split in order to join them in a temporary accomodation arranged for them by the board. They were also known as "the Mafia," an allusion to the high proportion of residents of Italian-American origins supposed to be among that group. Rumors abounded, some with staff encouragement, that members of this group were already "shooting dope." The function of such rumors obviously would be to deter other potential splittees and make residents cling more desperately to their present leaders in the very fearful situation in which they found themselves, as pawns in a power struggle between other forces, and involving issues which they could not possibly understand.

The board tried one last ploy before resorting to their ultimate legal weapon. They offered severance pay to staff if they would leave quietly. This was a tempting offer, especially to those with families to support and especially as the core group's efforts to find alternative accomodation and alternative funding sources had shown scant success. The offer was turned down. Deitch addressed meetings of residents designed to build up their confidence in his leadership, to assure them that they would all stay together in spite of the impending difficulties. He indulged in rhetoric of a distinctly prophetic tone, speaking of how they would all "pitch their tents together and break bread together," whatever may happen. At first the staff was disinclined to believe that the board really would go so far as to get an eviction order. As this possibility came to look more and more probable, the core group started making contingency plans and looking for alternative long-range sources of support. This was all within a very short space of time—at most a couple of weeks.

What the board wanted was for the staff loyal to Deitch to leave and for the residents to stay so that they could install the seven staff members loyal to them whom Deitch had earlier fired plus certain of the presently pro-Deitch staff who would come around to their side once he was out of the way and the Board was firmly in power. Deitch, however, had no intention of allowing this to happen. If he left, he would take the residents with him and leave empty houses for the board. They might control the funds and the physical facilities, but he would have the residents and "the soul of Daytop." He stated this openly.

Finally, the board obtained eviction orders and had them served on December 2 at each of the three houses. (By now a facility on 14th Street in Manhattan had been added to the original houses on Staten Island and at Swan Lake.) When the blow actually fell Deitch and his closest associates were on vacation in the Caribbean. Tearfully and with much distress, residents departed in three main parties for different places of refuge. Out of 183 residents in the houses, only eleven elected to remain. One group of the refugees went to New Haven, Connecticut, to an independent Daytop house founded by Daytop staff with an independent board (Daytop, Inc.); another group went to Rhode Island to Marathon House, another Concept house founded independently by Jim Germano, a former Daytop staff member; and the third group went to Philadelphia where a local committee had been already negotiating with Daytop staff to open a house there. The plan was that these places of refuge would be temporary, until David Deitch and the core group could find a new location and reunite everyone. But this never happened. They traveled from coast to coast but found nothing. So each of the three refugee groups settled down where they were. The Philadelphia group chose the name "Gaudenzia House" and the groups at Marathon House and Daytop Inc. were absorbed as members of these houses. Some of the refugees, of course, split. And of these, some returned to Daytop under the new administration.

Casriel was now executive director. Separate directors of administration and treatment were appointed. The latter was Ron Broncato, who had originally come from Synanon to Daytop as assistant to David Deitch, and who had been involved in an earlier unsuccessful attempt to have Deitch removed. He was director of the SPAN outreach project at the time of the crisis and it is surely significant that all of the SPAN staff sided with him and the board. This new regime at Daytop rapidly built up the resident population again, with splittees/returnees and fresh material. Six months after the evictions there were again 291 residents in Daytop.

The "big split" was a traumatic experience for all concerned—at least it was for the residents and staff. As for the board of directors, I have no information on this point. Six months later bitter feelings were still felt. There was bitterness on the part of the staff and residents at the board for evicting them. And in addition there was bitterness on the part of staff who led the refugee groups toward Deitch and those of the core group who went with him, who failed to keep their promise to reunite everyone in a new community. They did not even have the grace to inform their erstwhile followers but left it to others to draw the conclusion that the reunion would never occur and to break the news to the former Daytop residents in their new homes.

Deitch remarked at the height of the crisis, "I've learned a lot. I thought we could accept the establishment's money without accepting their rule." Perhaps it was not quite as simple as that, though. Perhaps the conflict was inherent in an organization under a lay board much more conservative in outlook than its full-time staff, a staff who sought to use the organization as a base for radical criticism of the secular society. But perhaps it need not have ended in such a destructive conflict. Perhaps, given a different executive director whose style was more conciliatory and less arrogant *vis-à-vis* his opponents on the board a *modus vivendi* could have been found which would have allowed most of what Deitch wanted, sacrificing only some of the more extravagant rhetoric.

When one attempts to specify in concrete terms exactly what Deitch or Daytop was doing that was so threatening to conservative interests in America, the list is not inconsequential but neither is it hair-raising in its revolutionary impact.

Daytop was operating SPAN offices in low-income neighborhoods of Manhattan to reach addicts and induct them into Daytop, to run groups for parents of residents and any other interested persons, and to attempt to mobilize local residents to improve the neighborhood by their own efforts and by putting pressure on city agencies, landlords, and others.

Daytop was running intensive training institutes mainly for members of the helping professions (also for the members of certain religious orders) in which they were challenged to confront their own situations more fully and to challenge their colleagues, subordinates, and bosses when they felt that they were not executing their responsibilities as they should.

Daytop was attempting in various ways to get the message to the wider public that in Daytop people were living a life based on honesty, concern, responsibility, and love; that people (former addicts, as it happens) of different age, sex, class, and ethnic backgrounds were living together in harmony as an extended family; and that, by contrast, the life of most other Americans was very much devoid of these qualities, though they professed to cherish the values. Attempts to get this message across were made through speaking engagements (though most of these tended to be limited to the "rehabilitation of addicts" theme), and through the play "The Concept," developed by Larry Sacharow and a group of Daytop residents and presented at an off-Broadway theater with great success.

Apparently there was disapproval among the board for the community action aspects of SPAN. Otherwise there was no serious dispute about the other projects just listed. Mainly it was the Deitch rhetoric and his behavior *vis-à-vis* the board itself which gave rise to the conflict. In other words, this conflict was one of personal feelings and was concerned with who should control Daytop. Was the legally empowered but distant board to have control? Or was the leader who breathed life into it and who was deeply and personally involved in it to have control?

An equilibrium was restored at Daytop in which the Board and the new staff settled down to a different kind of relationship, with the Board exercising greater control than before. Certain policies were also modified. Residents getting ready for reentry were encouraged to prepare themselves for jobs in the outside world unrelated to the treatment of addicts, if they wanted. Before the split, very few graduates had done this and a pressure had been developing that emphasized staying with Daytop as the ideal goal for a graduate. This was changed and so was the whole time scale on which residents advanced toward privileges and responsibilities.

The new staff maintained that residents had previously been kept down too long (including themselves)—to keep them dependent on Deitch and Daytop and hence available as cheap labor to staff the rapid expansion that occurred then. It is hard to know where the truth lay. Obviously the new Daytop administration was short of staff and were therefore tempted to push their residents ahead faster.

SOME WIDER IMPLICATIONS

Prior to 1969 Daytop had already begun to have an important impact in the fields of addict treatment, and human relations training. Since 1969 it would appear that these effects have continued, though in a somewhat different style. In concluding this analysis we must also take account of some important implications which can be seen to arise theoretically from what was being done in Daytop. Even though practical outcomes may not have developed from all the theoretical possibilities which have been demonstrated, it is still important to see what these theoretical implications are, for they may yet be coaxed into having practical results.

By far the most obvious and by no means the least important implication arising out of Daytop concerns the role of the ex-addict in the treatment and rehabilitation of other addicts. This is not an entirely new discovery, having been presaged by many years by the achievements of Alcoholics Anonymous (Maxwell, 1962). However, the principle of using the former sufferer to help the current one is taken a good deal further in Daytop. At the risk of oversimplifying, we may say that the distinction between the two approaches is that the AA approach is to persuade the alcoholic that he can live responsibly once he accepts that he has a serious problem, resolves never to drink another drop, and uses his AA group as an *emotional prop*, whereas the Daytop approach is to make the addict work on *changing* the underlying attitudes, and his methods of coping with fears and other problematic emotions.

Those who have been through the Daytop experience learn to deal with their own problems better and at the same time learn to give help to others in the various carefully-defined ways built into the culture of this therapeutic community. This raises an important point apropos the self-help group movement—that for a former sufferer to be an effective helper requires more than just having changed his own lifestyle. If requires some insight into the process of change and into the requirements of the helping role itself. Daytop teaches one version of such a process, as we have seen in some detail.

Between 1968, the time at which we studied Daytop, and 1972, when these observations were organized and written down, the use of paraprofessionals has become more accepted in many areas of work formerly reserved for professionally-trained personnel. No doubt Daytop has contributed in an important way to this increase in acceptance. Unfortunately much of this acceptance takes the form of a naive belief in the curative powers of the ex-addict (or the ex-prisoner for example). As we have indicated, the lesson of Daytop is that more than the bare fact of being an ex-addict is needed for a person to be an effective helper. He must have given up the values of the addict as well as just the behavior; he must be willing and able to practice *responsible* concern for the person he is supposed to be helping; he must be willing to relate to the changes he has been through honestly and not just to the extent that they are flattering to him; he must take a personal interest in his "client." Each of these requirements imply learning in a situation where the learner is supervised by more mature and experienced persons, a situation such as the Daytop one. He needs "training" and then continued supervision for a considerable time, something even Daytop house directors receive.

Turning to another implication, Daytop shows how the feelings of hostility and other interpersonal difficulties can be dealt with openly and directly to the great benefit of the individuals concerned and the climate of the group as a whole. Instead of holding on to resentments and grievances, which then become a growing impediment to functional relationships within the group, they can be dumped with all the vehemence they command in the controlled situation of the encounter group. This clears the air between the persons involved, enables them to look at the reasons for the difficulty arising, and enables them to work together better and to begin to become friends in some cases. It also undermines stereotyped and prejudiced interpersonal perceptions, enabling participants to see each other as individuals with good and bad points. Any group of people who work together or spend time together on a regular basis can probably benefit from such an arrangement, either at regular intervals or on a crisis basis. Already in the period when Daytop was under study various agencies in the human services area and several religious orders were sending members to Daytop for weekend Intensive Training Institutes.

Whereas virtually all the agencies, public and private alike, that purport to offer some kind of human helping service are organized and function bureaucratically, Daytop is successful because it takes the opposite approach. Traditional agencies and helping professions have become highly specialized, each offering an increasingly narrow range of help, so that each client must deal with several agencies and ends up feeling that none of them understands him properly or sees him as a *person.* Traditional agencies and helping professions generally deal with clients impersonally, applying universalistic standards as fairly as they can, and keeping their professional social distance from their clients. This may be an effective approach to matters of administration but it is surely not an effective way of influencing someone's attitudes or behavior.

By contrast the Daytop approach, as we have amply documented, is to create a communal or quasi-familial group in which each person is treated holistically—severely perhaps but certainly treated as a person. He is not treated by one specialist for one set of problems, then by another specialist for another set, and certainly is not bounced around between three or four specialists, as a hard-core client might well be in the traditional system of helping services. As he goes from an hour with Specialist One to his hour with Specialist Two and on to Specialist Three, he must necessarily repeat all the basic data concerning his problems for each specialist to abstract those facts which he deems pertinent in terms of his narrow interest in the client's case. Each specialist sees a vast number of clients, so even after several visits the client is well aware that he is perceived by those "helpers" as a *case* rather than an individual. Hence he feels alienated from these would-be helpers and from their efforts to change his attitudes and behavior.

In Daytop, by contrast, it is demanded of each resident that he approach other residents and talk about himself so that they may get to know him, and that he make efforts to get to know other residents. He is evaluated in terms of such criteria as honesty, openness, concern for others, and leadership—all criteria of a broad, moral, and functionally diffuse character—all related to him as a person rather than some specialized aspect of him.

Any special interest that a new resident may have, which may previously have been his life's obsession, he will at first be forbidden to engage in on the grounds that it enables him to avoid learning to be a better person in this sense.

The helping community that is Daytop, is premised on the assumption that drug addicts have never grown up in terms of emotional and moral development. Thus the function of Daytop is to give residents a second chance to grow up in this sense. Their period of residency is a recapitulation of their lost years. They are required to live under a regime of restrictions more appropriate to children or infants than to adults. And the rules under which they live are stated in absolute, harsh, black-and-white terms in much the same way as young children interpret the rules of society to be (Piaget 1932). Indeed the Daytop moral system is perhaps even more rigidly fundamentalist than that of early childhood, for it is being used to teach a sense of values to people who have (unlike the young child) already acquired a *warped* sense of values. Thus borrowing someone's pencil without first asking permission is defined as "stealing" in order to teach the meaning of honesty to people who could easily persuade themselves that, for example, taking a parent's painfully earned savings is all right.

The ethical fundamentalism of Daytop has other qualities besides this harsh rigor. It has a poignant beauty that shows itself especially clearly in the demonstrated human concern that is often seen between residents. In one instance observed after encounter groups one evening Charlie, who had just had a difficult time in his own group, was found sitting down with Don, who had just had his head shaved for reacting in his group. Three other male residents were also sitting in the same small room with them and the concentration of sympathy and concern that is focused on Don is intense. What Charlie was telling was very similar to what he was himself being told in his group an hour ago. "We're all the same," he told him, "we all have the same fears, the same feelings. . . ." He said it with feeling and Don had tears in his eyes, not tears of self-pity, but tears forced out by the intensity of emotion. He had been able to let it out, thanks to the trust he feels in these peers evoked by their evident concern. Charlie also feels better: he seems to have grown an inch or two in pride and humanity.

Daytop has the power to generate tremendous excitement in visitors. Of course, what they see at first is more of its tender side and less of the tough understructure which necessarily goes with it. Even when they do begin to get a more balanced view, Daytop frequently continues to fascinate and attract. All are not necessarily attracted by the same features. What attracts some is the communal nature of the group and the insititutionalized altruism; what attracts others is the struggle of so many individuals to make better persons of themselves; to others it may be the orderliness and discipline; and to yet others it may be the sense of security they find in this tightly-organized communal group with its strong collective goals.

In a remarkable way, Daytop, Synanon and the "Concept House" therapeutic communities which have followed the same model have managed to combine elements in Western culture which have hitherto been mostly at war with each other. One of these elements, sometimes labeled "the Protestant Ethic," may be defined as the notion that man should strive to overcome any obstacles to his ambitions lying either in the physical environment or within himself in the form of a personal weakness or handicap (Weber, 1958). To resign oneself to accept hardships or difficulties is held to be dishonorable whereas to struggle to overcome them is praiseworthy—even if the cost is high or the struggle eventually unsuccessful. This ethic is a central feature of North American culture. Most commonly, though, it has come to be understood in a narrow and materialistic sense and to involve evaluating people on the basis of wealth and other outward signs of material success.

The second of these cultural values is altruism, or the obligation to show concern for each other. This value has always been a major element in the Judaeo-Christian humanistic tradition of the West, though it has historically been thoroughly subordinated to the value of material success.

The hippie movement has attracted thousands of young people who reject the American version of the Protestant Ethic and choose to drop out of the lifestyle of the middle class to embrace a way of life supposedly oriented towards altruism and personal autonomy (and drugs), and rejecting the worship of material things. (Yablonsky, 1968; Roszak, 1969).

The Concept House movement, too, rejects the materialism of modern America, not only the emphasis on material success but also the emphasis on "externals" such as lifestyle, status symbols, wealth, fame, and so forth. Instead it upholds the values of altruism or concern, honesty, and responsibility—essentially "internal" or "moral" qualities by contrast with the external features more commonly emphasized. Yet, unlike the hippies, the Concept House movement does not totally reject the Protestant Ethic. On the contrary, it embodies a very strong commitment to the notion that each person has the responsibility of overcoming his problems so that he can lead a responsible life.

This is more in line with the original concept of "the Protestant Ethic" though it is at variance with the more recent American version of that ethic. What the Concept Houses have achieved, therefore, is a new synthesis of the two main elements of the value system of modern civilization which have previously been in conflict with each other. To have brought together again the emphasis on mastery of one's own life situation and the value of altruism is a remarkable achievement. It is an achievement of profoundly important implications, which explains to a significant extent the fascination that Synanon, Daytop, *et al.* have exercised over many visitors.

For many people who are not residents of these remarkable communities and who find neither the mainstream materialism of America nor the hippie lifestyle acceptable, the Concept synthesis represents an alternative set of value commitments. The main credit for this, as for so many of the features of Daytop which we have described, belongs to Synanon, the originator of this social movement. The Daytop of this period made some modifications in the Synanon model but not in its essentials.

Deitch's Daytop was, in its time, the best program available for drug addicts but it was not, of course, perfect. Arguably, it grew too big, losing a lot of the real family feeling of the early days and the very close relationships that residents could once have with staff. In addition, staff expertise became diluted in relation to the number of residents. It can also be argued that too little was done to help residents in the reentry phase to learn to operate outside of the house, so they could make a real choice, whether to stay or leave after graduation.

Despite these criticisms, the Daytop of this period was a great landmark in the field of drug addict rehabilitation. Those who were part of Deitch's Daytop felt that they were involved in a movement that was going to have a major impact on the larger society. This was an intoxicating feeling for people who had only recently been social outcasts.

The Concept House movement lives on, through the now numerous Houses that try in their different styles to follow the principles we have examined in this case study. There is old mother Synanon, who began it all; there is Daytop, now without the brilliant but reckless leadership of David Deitch; there is Phoenix House, the large New York City program, started with Daytop help and initially staffed with former Synanon personnel. Among the third generation is Odyssey House, a successful partnership of professional and ex-addict staff (with the latter subordinate), and a group of houses run by former Daytop associates of Deitch including Daytop, Inc., Gaudenzia House, Gateway House, Renaissance House, and Marathon House. There is also a fourth generation of houses run by staff who themselves graduated (or split) from some of the earlier houses.

On a superficial level all the houses belonging to the Concept movement can be identified by certain external characteristics: they are run by ex-addicts; a tight discipline is maintained in a drug-free, self-help group, enforced with the use of pull-ups, haircuts, group encounters, and so forth. The real point is, though, that these are merely *means* that have been found useful as part of a process of helping people to learn a new way of life. That way of life is defined by the principle that human relations can be based on honesty between people and responsible concern for each other—a concept much preached in Western civilization, but seldom practiced; a concept that has seldom been institutionalized anywhere as successfully as it has been in these communities of the Concept.

References

Casriel, Daniel, 1963, *So Fair A House.* Englewood Cliffs, N.J.: Prentice-Hall.
———, 1966, "A Modification of Adaptational Psychodynamic Theory in the Wake of Successful Treatment of the Drug Addict at Daytop Village." Paper presented at the Annual Meeting of the American Psychiatric Association at Atlantic City, N.J., May 1966.
Casriel, Daniel, and Amen, Grover, 1971, *Daytop: Three Lives.* New York: Hill and Wang.
Deitch, David A., 1973, "Treatment of Drug Abuse in the Therapeutic Community," in *Technical Papers of the Second Report of the National Commission on Marijuana and Drug Abuse*, Appendix, Vol. IV, pp. 158–175.
Endore, Guy, 1968, *Synanon.* New York: Doubleday.
Fort, John P., Jr., 1966, "Heroin Addiction among Young Men" in O'Donnell and Ball (eds.), *op. cit.*
O'Donnell, John A., and Ball, John C., (eds.), 1966, *Narcotic Addiction.* New York: Harper & Row.
Goffman, Erving, 1961, *Asylums.* Garden City, N.Y.: Doubleday.
Joint Committee of the American Medical Association and American Bar Association, 1963, "Drug Addiction: Crime or Disease?" in Dan Wakefield (ed.), *The Addict.* Greenwich, Conn.: Fawcett, p. 9.
Maxwell, Milton A., 1962, "Alcoholics Anonymous: An Interpretation," in David J. Pittman and C. R. Snyder (eds.), *Society, Culture, and Drinking Patterns.* New York: Wiley.
Mills, James, 1966, "The World of Needle Park" in O'Donnell and Ball (eds.), *op. cit.*
National Institute of Mental Health, 1963, *Narcotic Drug Addiction.* Mental Health Monograph No. 2, Bethesda, Md.: NIMH. Quotations from p. 11 and p. 6, respectively.
———, *Directory of Narcotic Addiction Treatment Agencies in the U.S. 1968–1969*, P.H.S. Publication No. 2095.
Piaget, Jean, 1932, *Moral Judgment of the Child.* London: Routledge.
Pilati, Joe, 1968, "The Daytop Explosion: Addiction to Power," *Village Voice*, Nov. 21, 1968.
Roszak, Theodore, 1969, *The Making of a Counter Culture.* New York: Doubleday.
Shelly, Joseph A., 1969, Final Report on Daytop Lodge (MH 1292 and 2583), submitted to NIMH (mimeo).
Sugarman, Barry, 1967, "Daytop Village: A Drug-Cure Cooperative." *New Society*, April 13, 1967, pp. 526–529.
———, 1973, *The School and Moral Development.* New York: Barnes & Noble.
Vaillent, George E., 1966, "A Twelve-Year Follow-Up of New York Narcotic Addicts: The Relation of Treatment to Outcome," *American Journal of Psychiatry*, 1966, pp. 727–737.
Weber, Max, 1958, *The Protestant Ethic and the Spirit of Capitalism*, translated by T. Parsons. New York: Scribner.

Wheeler, Stanton, 1966, "The Structure of Formally Organized Socialization Settings," in Orville G. Brim, Jr., and Stanton Wheeler (eds.), *Socialization after Childhood.* New York: Wiley.

Yablonsky, Lewis, 1965, *Synanon: The Tunnel Back.* Baltimore, Md.: Penguin.

———, 1968, *The Hippie Trip.* New York: Pegasus.